rockschool®

Guitar

US Level 8 (UK Grade 8)

Performance pieces, technical exercises and in-depth guidance for Rockschool assessments

All accompanying and supporting audio can be downloaded from: *www.rslawards.com/downloads*

Input the following code when prompted: **4QB6PDRTKH**

For more information, turn to page 4

www.rslawards.com

Acknowledgements

Published by Rockschool Ltd. © 2012, 2018 & 2020
Catalogue Number: RSK200050US
ISBN: 978-1-78936-146-9
Initial US Release | Errata details can be found at *www.rslawards.com/errata*

CONTACTING ROCKSCHOOL
www.rslawards.com
Telephone: +44 (0)345 460 4747
Email: *info@rslawards.com*

Syllabus Director
Tim Bennett-Hart

Head of Graded Music & Publishing
Jono Harrison

2018 Syllabus Repertoire
Produced by Nik Preston

Proof reading
Sharon Kelly, Calum Harrison, Jono Harrison, Nik Preston
(and all arrangers/performers)

US Book Editions (2020)
Additional design work by Steven Price (51 Degrees Design)
and Simon Troup (Digital Music Art)
Edited by Jennie Troup (Digital Music Art)

Syllabus Consultants (Hit Tunes 2018 Repertoire)
Guitar: James Betteridge, Andy G Jones
Bass: Joe Hubbard, Diego Kovadloff, Joel McIver
Drums: Paul Elliott, Pete Riley

Arrangers (Hit Tunes 2018 Repertoire)
Guitar: James Betteridge, Andy G Jones, Mike Goodman, Viv Lock
Bass: Diego Kovadloff, Andy Robertson, Joe Hubbard
Drums: Paul Elliott, Stu Roberts, Pete Riley

Publishing (Hit Tunes 2018 Repertoire)
Fact files by Diego Kovadloff
Covers designed by Phil Millard (Rather Nice design)
Music engraving, internal design and layout by
Simon Troup & Jennie Troup (Digital Music Art)

Distribution
Exclusive Distributors: Hal Leonard

Musicians (Hit Tunes 2018 Repertoire)
Guitar: Andy G Jones, James Betteridge, Mike Goodman,
          David Rhodes (Peter Gabriel)
Bass: Nik Preston, Joe Hubbard, Stuart Clayton,
          Andy Robertson, John Illsley (Dire Straits)
Drums: Paul Elliott, Pete Riley, Peter Huntington, Stu Roberts,
          Billy Cobham (Miles Davis, Mahavishnu Orchestra)
Vocals: Kim Chandler
Keys: Jono Harrison, Hannah V (on 'Red Baron'), Andy Robertson
Horns: Tom Walsh (tpt), Martin Williams (sax), Andy Wood (trmb)

Recording & Audio Engineering (Hit Tunes 2018 Repertoire)
Recording engineers: Oli Jacobs, Scott Barnett, Patrick Phillips
Mixing engineer: Samuel Vasanth
Mastering engineer: Samuel Vasanth
Audio production: Nik Preston
Audio management: Ash Preston, Samuel Vasanth
Recording studios: Real World Studios, The Premises

Publishing (Rockschool 2012 Repertoire)
Fact Files written by Joe Bennett, Charlie Griffiths, Stephen Lawson,
Simon Pitt, Stuart Ryan and James Uings
Walkthroughs written by James Uings
Music engraving, internal design and layout by
Simon Troup & Jennie Troup (Digital Music Art)
Proof reading and copy editing by Chris Bird, Claire Davies, Stephen
Lawson, Simon Pitt and James Uings
Publishing administration by Caroline Uings
Additional drum proof reading by Miguel Andrews

Instrumental Specialists (Rockschool 2012 Repertoire)
Guitar: James Uings
Bass: Stuart Clayton
Drums: Noam Lederman

Musicians (Rockschool 2012 Repertoire)
Andy Crompton, Camilo Tirado, Carl Sterling, Charlie Griffiths,
Chris Webster, Dave Marks, DJ Harry Love, Felipe Karam,
Fergus Gerrand, Henry Thomas, Jake Painter, James Arben,
James Uings, Jason Bowld, Joe Bennett, Jon Musgrave, Kishon Khan,
Kit Morgan, Larry Carlton, Neel Dhorajiwala, Nir Z, Noam Lederman,
Norton York, Richard Pardy, Ross Stanley, Simon Troup, Steve Walker,
Stuart Clayton, Stuart Ryan

Recording & Audio Engineering (Rockschool 2012 Repertoire)
Recorded at The Farm (Fisher Lane Studios)
Produced and engineered by Nick Davis
Assistant engineer and Pro Tools operator Mark Binge
Mixed and mastered at Langlei Studios
Mixing and additional editing by Duncan Jordan
Supporting Tests recorded by Duncan Jordan and Kit Morgan
Mastered by Duncan Jordan
Executive producers: James Uings, Jeremy Ward and Noam Lederman

Executive Producers
John Simpson, Norton York

RSL Awarding the Contemporary Arts

Table of Contents

Introductions & Information

1	Title Page
2	Acknowledgements
3	Table of Contents
4	Welcome to Rockschool Guitar Level/Grade 8

Hit Tunes

5	Snarky Puppy	'Native Sons'
11	Steve Vai	'Die to Live'
17	Steely Dan	'Kid Charlemagne'
23	D'Angelo	'Spanish Joint'
29	Justin Timberlake	'Cry Me A River (Live iTunes Festival 2013)'
35	Albert Lee	'Country Boy'

Rockschool Originals

43	'Meet Darth Ear'
49	'Mind The Gaps'
55	'Lead Sheet'
61	'Freightshaker'
67	'Nosso Samba'
73	'Dark Matter'

Technical Exercises

79	Scales, Arpeggios, Chords & Stylistic Studies

Supporting Tests

85	Quick Study Piece
88	Ear Tests
89	General Musicianship Questions

Additional Information

90	Entering Rockschool Assessments
91	Marking Schemes
92	Introduction to Tone
94	Guitar Notation Explained
95	Mechanical Copyright Information
96	Rockschool Popular Music Theory

Welcome to Rockschool Guitar Level/Grade 8

Welcome to Guitar Level/Grade 8
Welcome to the **Rockschool 2018 Guitar syllabus**. This book and the accompanying downloadable audio contain everything you need to play guitar at this level/grade. In the book you will find the scores in both standard guitar notation and TAB, as well as Fact Files and Walkthroughs for each song.
The downloadable audio includes:
- full stereo mixes of six Rockschool compositions and six arrangements of classic and contemporary hits
- backing tracks (minus the assessed guitar part)
- all necessary audio for the complete range of supporting tests

Guitar Assessments
At each level/grade, you have the option of taking one of two different types of assessment:

- **Level/Grade Assessment:** a Level/Grade Assessment is a mixture of music performances, technical work and tests. You prepare three pieces (two of which may be Free Choice Pieces) and the contents of the Technical Exercise section. This accounts for 75% of the assessment marks. The other 25% consists of: a Quick Study Piece (10%), a pair of instrument specific Ear Tests (10%), and finally you will be asked five General Musicianship Questions (5%). The pass mark is 60%.

- **Performance Certificate:** in a Performance Certificate you play five pieces. Up to three of these can be Free Choice Pieces. Each song is marked out of 20 and the pass mark is 60%.

Book Contents
The book is divided into a number of sections. These are:

- **Assessment Pieces:** in this book you will find six specially commissioned pieces of Level/Grade 8 standard. Each of these is preceded by a *Fact File*. Each Fact File contains a summary of the song, including the style, tempo, key and technical features, along with a list of the musicians who played on it. The song is printed on up to four pages. Immediately after each song is a *Walkthrough*. This covers the song from a performance perspective, focusing on the technical issues you will encounter along the way. Each song comes with a full mix version and a backing track. Both versions have spoken count-ins at the beginning. Please note that any solos played on the full mix versions are indicative only.

- **Technical Exercises:** you should prepare the exercises set in this level/grade in the keys indicated. You should also choose *one* Stylistic Study from the three printed to practise and play to the backing track in the assessment. The style you choose will determine the style of the Quick Study Piece.

- **Supporting Tests and General Musicianship Questions:** in Guitar Level/Grade 8 there are three supporting tests – a Quick Study Piece, a pair of Ear Tests and a set of General Musicianship Questions (GMQs) asked at the end of each assessment. Examples of the types of tests likely to appear in the assessment are printed in this book. Additional examples of both types of test and the GMQs can be found in the Rockschool *Guitar Companion Guide*.

- **Additional Information:** finally, you will find information on assessment procedures, marking schemes, guitar tone and guitar notation.

Audio
Audio is provided in the form of backing tracks (minus guitar) and examples (including guitar) for the pieces and the supporting tests where applicable. Audio files are supplied in MP3 format to enable playback on a wide range of compatible devices. Digital versions of the book include audio files in the download. Download audio for hardcopy books from RSL directly at *www.rslawards.com/downloads* — you will need to input this code when prompted: **4QB6PDRTKH**

Syllabus Guide
All candidates should read the accompanying syllabus guide when using this level/grade book. This can be downloaded from the RSL website: *www.rslawards.com*

Errata
Updates and changes to Rockschool books are documented online. Candidates should check for errata periodically while studying for any assessment. Further details can be found on the RSL website: *www.rslawards.com/errata*

Snarky Puppy

SONG TITLE: NATIVE SONS
ALBUM: THE WORLD IS GETTING SMALLER
LABEL: ROPEADOPE RECORDS
GENRE: JAZZ FUSION

WRITTEN BY: MICHAEL LEAGUE
PRODUCED BY: MICHAEL LEAGUE

US CHART PEAK: N/A

BACKGROUND INFO

'Native Sons' is a composition by bassist Michael League included on Snarky Puppy's 2007 release *The World is Getting Smaller*. The recording features guitarists Bob Lanzetti and Chris McQueen who are long standing members of Snarky Puppy.

Chris McQueen also plays with jazz fusion quartet Forq, indie band Foe Destroyer and world-music group Bokanté. He also transcribes Snarky Puppy's material for sheet music production and plays in an acoustic guitar duo with Matt Read. McQueen has worked on several rock musicals including David Bowie's *Lazarus* and the *Rocky Horror Show*. He built the iPhone app Guitar Note Atlas.

Bob Lanzetti is based in New York City. He released *Whose Feet are These That are Walking?*, recorded with his quintet, for which he composed and produced all the material. He also composed the score for two dance films for the Allendance Company and performed improvised solo guitar for yoga and dance classes. Lanzetti teaches in his studio in Brooklyn and works in outreach programmes for underprivileged teens through the Carnegie Hall. He is also a member of Bokanté. As a sideman he has worked with Cory Henry, Tommy Sims and Underground System amongst many others.

Michael League is a force to be reckoned with. Not only is he a fantastic bass player, composer and producer but he is also a very smart and able promoter, who realised early on that the visual presence of the band was as important as its studio production if it was going to reach a young audience. He reached a generation of listeners whose first contact with much music is via YouTube. His visual approach is a no nonsense one – the band is filmed playing live, they do so exceptionally well, and as a consequence the band have been touring the world non-stop for over a decade. Snarky Puppy is a vast assembly of musicians, some more permanent than others, many of whom were former University of North Texas students. The band won three Grammy Awards and are signed to Universal Records. Snarky Puppy has collaborated with many musicians including Metropole Orchestra, Jacob Collier, David Crosby and Charlie Hunter.

Native Sons

Snarky Puppy
Words & Music by Michael League

♩=121 *Jazz Fusion*

Walkthrough

Amp Settings

The sound needs to be fairly clean for the melodic parts but you could add more overdrive or distortion for the solo. A little reverb wouldn't go amiss. The basic sound should have a little bluesy grit to it. A wash of delay could be added for the solo.

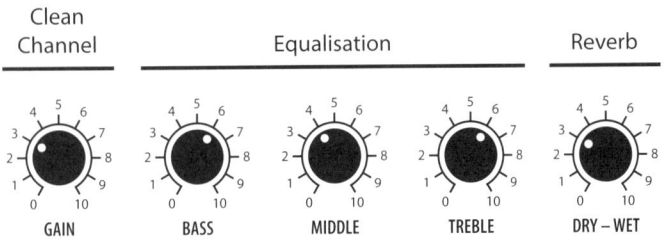

A Section (Measures 9–22)

This is a funky line which doubles the bassline. There are no other instruments providing backing so the harmony isn't clear here. The rhythm is very syncopated and as the drums haven't started playing (just the percussion is playing here) it's a little more difficult to feel the pulse. You need to prepare this section carefully but it's worth the effort.

Measure 9

The first note the guitar plays is on the second 16th note of beat 3. It would be easy to lose your place on the beat but this is what preparation time is for. Count hard when the intro starts and try and internalise the passing of the beats. Try tapping your foot on beats 2 and 4. Try alternate picking but some players might use the right hand middle finger to pick the open G string before making the leap down to the low G with the pick.

B Section (Measures 23–34)

In this section the drums have joined in, which makes feeling the pulse much easier. The notes are basically the same as in Section A.

C Section (Measures 35–48)

This section is mostly less active than the previous two. However, you should plan your picking approach for the little single note fill in measure 36. Planning right hand picking is easily as important as planning left hand fingering, so it's worth experimenting until you find the approach that works for you.

Measure 45

In this measure the arrangement covers the melody, while adding chords where possible. This approach is useful in a small band where harmony instruments or a horn section are missing.

Solo Section (Measures 80–94)

This is a shorter version of the solo on the album. The changes firstly cycle around a three chord pattern – Am^7, B^7 and F major^7. A minor and F major^7 are in the same area harmonically. A natural minor has the same notes as F Lydian (Lydian is the same as a major scale but with the fourth degree raised a semitone). The B^7 chord is somewhat unexpected – this is outside the A minor harmonic orbit. This is the kind of modern jazz influenced harmony that works by voice leading. Note how the bottom two notes of the Am^7 voicing move down by a semitone to create the B^7 chord – this is reminiscent of Steely Dan. This is not necessarily about functional harmony – for example, B^7 is not a secondary dominant of the next chord F major^7. The notes used over the B^7 chord should reflect the harmonic environment – the key centre could be seen as A minor so it's a good idea to use C natural (the flat 9th) rather than C♯ (the major 9th) over the root B.

Measures 89–94

Here the harmony changes. The $Dadd^2/F\sharp$ could be seen as a D^7 first inversion. At first glance this could be seen as an unusual chord, but if the Am^7 that started this section used the A Dorian mode the notes of D^7 would be contained in that scale. Am^7 and D^7 are very closely related and form a II-V chord pattern. Over the E^7sus^4 try B Dorian or B minor pentatonic as your first option.

You'll find that when improvising over a new tune you'll need to live with it for a while. It can be surprising how quickly ideas start coming when you take time to experiment. When you come up with an idea you like, write it down for future reference.

Steve Vai

SONG TITLE: DIE TO LIVE
ALBUM: ALIEN LOVE SECRETS EP
LABEL: RELATIVITY
GENRE: INSTRUMENTAL ROCK

WRITTEN BY: STEVE VAI
PRODUCED BY: STEVE VAI

US CHART PEAK: N/A

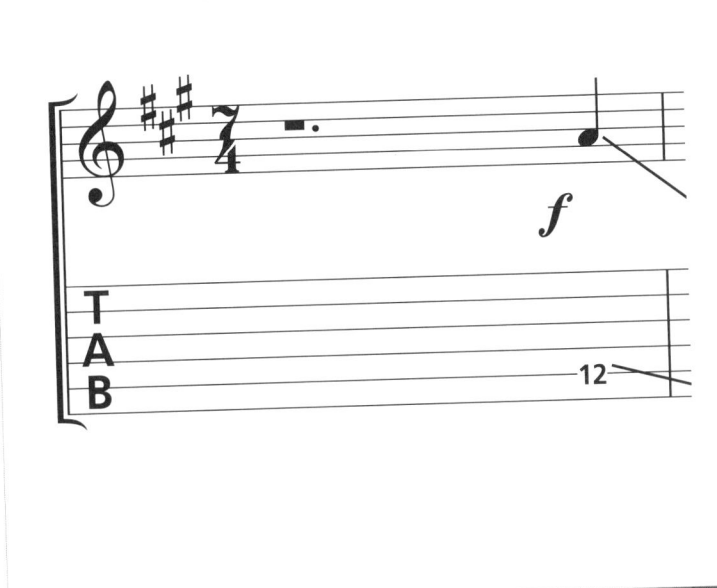

BACKGROUND INFO

Steve Vai released the *Alien Love Secrets* EP whilst recording *Fire Garden*, the follow up to his 1993 release *Sex and Religion*. The planned recording of over 70 minutes of music was taking too long so Vai decided to release an EP as an advance of the LP.

Steve Vai is a highly acclaimed guitarist known for his impeccably fluid technique and individual style. He started out doing transcriptions of Zappa's work in 1978, and subsequently joined Zappa's band in 1980, working with him until 1983. His ability to notate music was outstanding and he managed to score material that Zappa himself had difficulty in notating, although he played it. Much of this included the use of unusual tuplets, typical in contemporary classical music. Upon leaving Zappa's band he released *Flex-Able* and gradually established himself at the top of the pyramid in the world of virtuosic rock playing that gained popularity in the 1980s.

Steve Vai won three Grammy Awards and has worked with Alcatrazz, David Lee Roth, Whitesnake, Mary J. Blige, Spinal Tap, and Ozzy Osbourne. He has toured as a solo artist and with live-only acts G3, Zappa Plays Zappa and The Experience Hendrix Tour. Vai has released eight solo albums to date.

Steve Vai decided to start playing the guitar upon hearing Jimmy Page's solo on Led Zeppelin's 'Heartbreaker'. He counts Jimmy Page, Brian May, Jeff Beck, Ritchie Blackmore, Jimi Hendrix, Allan Holdsworth and Al Di Meola as his major influences. Vai attended the Berklee College of Music to study theory and composition but left to work with Zappa after four semesters. He was awarded an Honorary Doctorate of Music from Berklee in 2000.

Steve Vai started taking lessons with Joe Satriani aged 13 and developed a strict work ethic that he adheres to today. He is a committed educator and as such he has held touring masterclasses which include open discussions and improvisation with attendees. Vai has a set of beliefs that relate music to more esoteric principles which he articulates in a singular and heartfelt fashion. He is a devoted practitioner of meditation, an avid reader of spiritual and religious literature, a vegetarian and beekeeper. He works from his home studio, The Harmony Hut, located in the backyard of his house in Los Angeles.

Die to Live

Steve Vai
Music by Steve Vai

† Tapped harmonic:
Fret notes as indicated in tablature and tap strings
above fret indicated between the staves

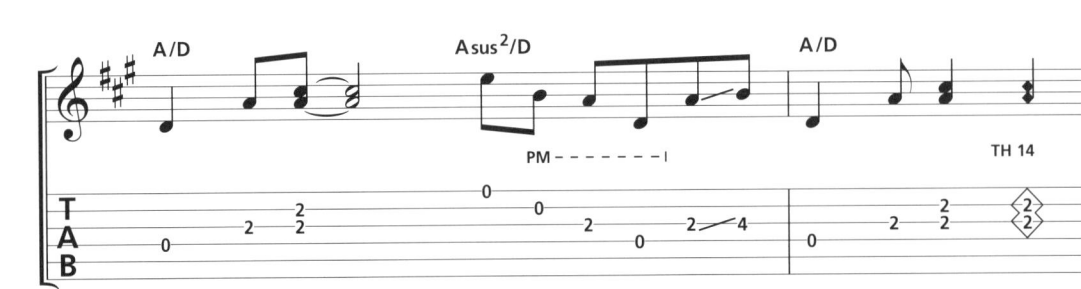

© Copyright 1995 Sy Vy Music.
Carlin Music Corporation.
All Rights Reserved. International Copyright Secured.

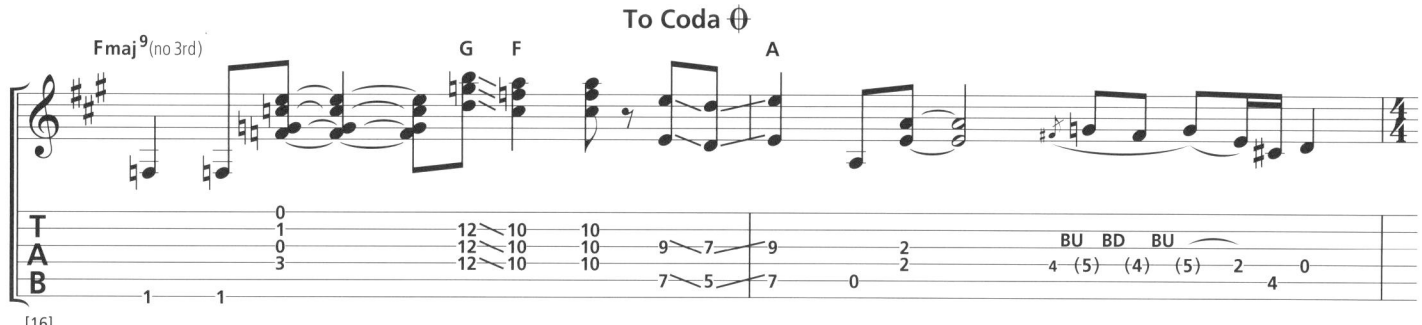

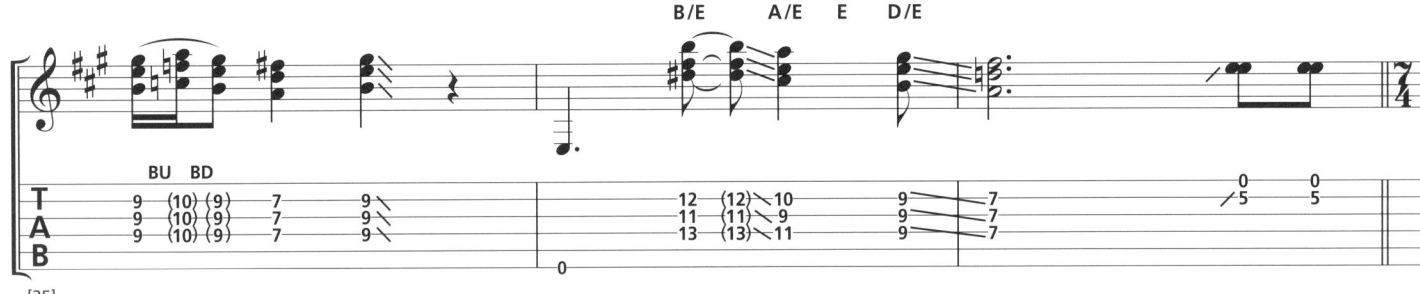

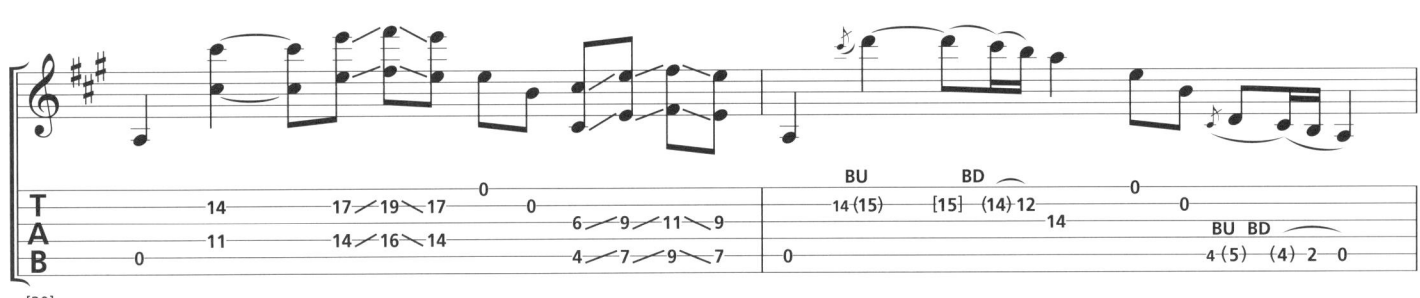

Walkthrough

Amp Settings

Note that these settings are just suggestions. Depending on the guitar and amplifier you play through, these settings will change! You may want to consider putting a distortion unit in front of the amp to help achieve the required sound. Essentially this piece requires a heavily distorted guitar sound, bright with a lot of mids. A guitar fitted with humbuckers is preferable to achieve a similar sound to the recording. Experiment with EQ on your amp/effects unit and, most importantly, make sure you are happy your sound!

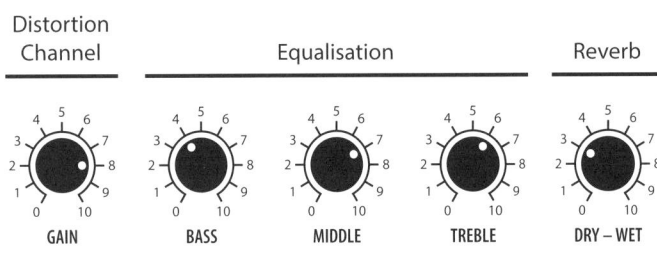

Intro

This piece is in 7/4 and in the key of A major. The intro starts with just the guitar playing an arpeggiated figure based around an A major and $Asus^2$ chords, played in open position. Notice the tap harmonics on the 'and' of beat 3 in measure 2. These require you to tap on the 12th fret (1 octave) above the note fretted. If you are not used to playing in odd time signatures it might be a good idea to spend time just listening to the piece, and the original track, to get accustomed to the feel of the odd time signature. You may also find it useful to count each measure as a measure of 4 and 3 beats instead of counting to 7 each measure. Take note of the palm muted notes in the measures indicated.

A Section

The rhythm section enters at the A section, with the guitar continuing to play the same melodic motif, with 'call and response' phrases on every other measure. At measure 10 the harmony changes to the IV chord ($Dmaj^7$) for 2 measures before returning to the tonic (A). As the guitar part is very 'exposed' against the drums and bass, it's worth spending some time becoming comfortable with all the variations and subtleties of each phrase, as Steve Vai's unique sense of phrasing and articulation can be quite a challenge.

At measure 14 the harmony changes again to a G^5/C and then an $Fmaj^7(sus^2)$ chord. This Modal interchange can be seen as the $\flat 3$ and 4 chords, 'borrowed' from the parallel key of A minor. At measure 18 the time signature changes from 7/4 to 4/4, with the guitar playing long held notes. The challenge with this part of the piece is to let the notes ring out whilst navigating the changes.

B Section

The B section is a repeat of the A section form with the guitar part developing on the original melody. There are frequent large shifts in positions in this section which will take a little getting used to. As an example spend time working on the transitions between the 'Tapped' notes, in the first half of measures 28 and 29, and the open arpeggiated chords in the second half of each measure, as this can be challenging at tempo. Take the *D.S. al Coda* at the end of this section, back to the sign at the beginning of section A, and play through until you reach the *To Coda* marking at the end of section B.

Coda Section

The *Coda* section begins with a chordal figure, A to $Asus^4$, then to the 6 chord ($F\sharp m^{11}$) and finishing on the $\flat 7$ chord (G^5), before finally resolving back to the tonic (A). The guitar finishes with an arpeggiated figure on $Asus^2$.

Steely Dan

SONG TITLE: KID CHARLEMAGNE
ALBUM: THE ROYAL SCAM
LABEL: ABC
GENRE: JAZZ ROCK / POP ROCK / JAZZ FUSION

WRITTEN BY: DONALD FAGEN AND WALTER BECKER
PRODUCED BY: GARY KATZ

US CHART PEAK: 82

BACKGROUND INFO

In 1972, producer Gary Katz hired the duo of Donald Fagen and Walter Becker as staff songwriters upon moving to LA to work for ABC. The complexity of their songs led Katz to suggest the duo form their own band to perform them, and that led to the creation of Steely Dan. Katz produced all of their records and Roger Nichols engineered them, earning six Grammy Awards as a result. The band enjoyed success but, tired from touring, Fagen and Becker decided to concentrate solely on songwriting and studio work by the end of 1974. This opened the door to what became their golden era.

In 1975 Steely Dan recorded *Katy Lied* with a rotating cast of session musicians, a process they used from that point onwards. Their writing became more sophisticated musically and lyrically, going on to record *The Royal Scam* (1976), *Aja* (1977) and *Gaucho* (1980). The latter two records are regarded as unique masterpieces.

'Kid Charlemagne' was included on *The Royal Scam* and released as a single in May 1976. It reached no.82 on the Billboard charts, achieving critical acclaim and classic status through its blend of funk, rock and jazz – coupled with the duo's unique lyrical style. This song features a renowned guitar solo by guitarist Larry Carlton, one which is widely regarded as a landmark in contemporary guitar playing. The unique groove of this track was provided by Don Grolnick (Fender Rhodes), Paul Griffin (clavinet), Chuck Rainey (bass) and Bernard Purdie (drums).

Larry Carlton's guitar work is amongst the most significant in popular music. His unique blend of sophisticated harmony, tasteful and narrative solos, and deep understanding of the song as a vehicle for expression through his instrument saw him grace the work of Steely Dan, Joni Mitchell, The Crusaders, Robben Ford and Fourplay, as well thousands of recordings (including over one hundred gold records). He also recorded a number of successful solo albums in his home studio, *Room 335*, named after the Gibson ES-335 he often played.

Kid Charlemagne

Steely Dan
Words & Music by Donald Fagen & Walter Becker

© Copyright 1976 ABC Dunhill Music Incorporated.
Universal/MCA Music Limited.
All Rights Reserved. International Copyright Secured.

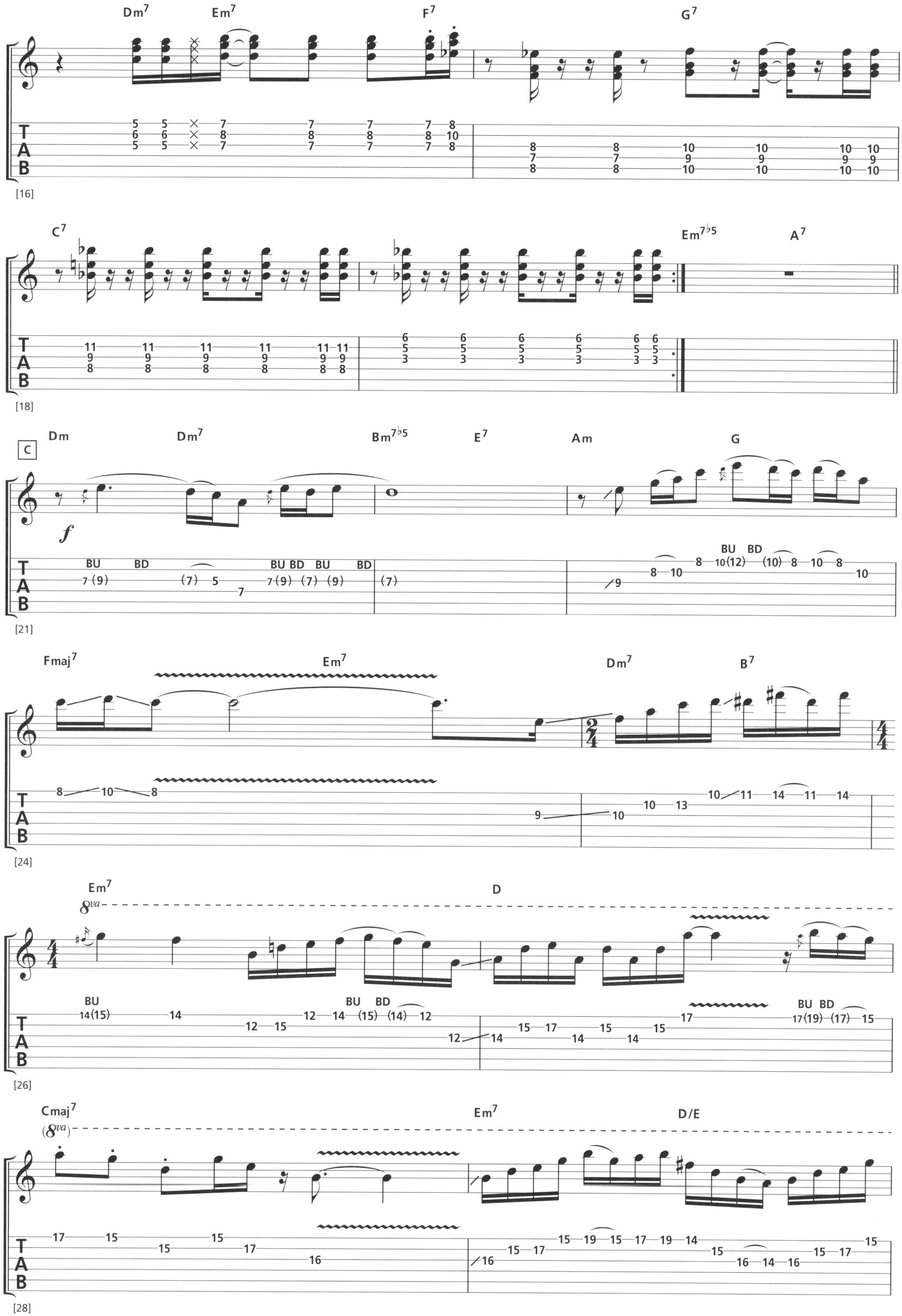
Dm7 Em7 F7 G7
[16]
C7 Em7♭5 A7
[18]
C
Dm Dm7 Bm7♭5 E7 Am G
[21]
Fmaj7 Em7 Dm7 B7
[24]
Em7 D
[26]
Cmaj7 Em7 D/E
[28]

Walkthrough

Amp Settings

Larry Carlton used a Gibson 335 on the bridge pickup through a tweed deluxe amplifier for this track. The guitar tone for the rhythm parts isn't completely clean and has a slight 'bite' to the sound. Maybe set the drive channel on a low setting, allowing for a slight 'crunchy' sound. Another option is to set the amp for the solo sound and use the volume control on the guitar to 'clean' up the sound for the rhythm parts.

Note that the EQ levels above are just suggestions. Depending on the guitar and amplifier you play through these settings will change. Experiment with pickup selection and tone settings on your guitar to see what different tonal colours you like and feel suit the sound of the song the best.

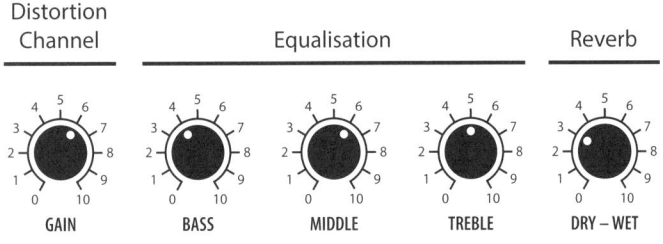

A Section

The song is in the key of A minor and this abridged arrangement jumps straight into the verse section, with a 16th-note rhythm figure played through the changes, Am (I), G^6 ($\flat$VII), $F^{6/9}$ ($\flat$VI), $B\flat^{13}$ (tri-tone substitution of E^7) chords.

B Section

The B section introduces a new chord progression with the inclusion of Dm^7 (iv) and Em^7 (v) chords. Notice that all the chord voicings are small, utilising a couple of strings at a time. Be careful not to let any unwanted string ring out here. At the end of this section take the repeat back to the beginning of section A.

C Section (Solo)

Before you jump straight into the solo itself it's a good idea to look at the chord progression the solo is played over to get a better understanding of the scale choices. The pickup into the solo (measure 20) is a minor ii–V resolving to the Dm^7 (chord iv in the overarching key of A minor).

This classic solo starts with the A minor pentatonic scale, over the iv chord Dm^7. Measure 25 is a 2/4 measure (Dm^7 to B^7) – notice the B^7 (a secondary dominant) leading into the Em chord in the next measure (26). Larry manages to mirror this change in the solo by playing D min pentatonic on the first beat of the measure, then sliding a semitone from D to D♯, (major 3rd of B^7) on beat 2. The solo then modulates to E minor, moving to D ($\flat$VII) then $Cmaj^7$ ($\flat$VI) until measure 29, where the D/E (IV/V of Am) takes us back to the key of A minor. Notice, in measure 29, the use of triads to subtly navigate the Em to D/E chord change. At measure 30 the changes mirror those of the chords in the verse section, until measure 38 where there are 4 measures of C^7 (secondary dominant). Here the solo outlines the C mixolydian scale over the C^7 chord. The 'infamous' tapped note is in measure 41, where the major 3rd is played and the $\flat 7$ (B$\flat$) is tapped at the 14th fret. This solo is a great lesson in the use of triads when soloing, and there are lots of great ideas to 'steal' and use in your own playing!

D Section

The D section returns to the verse form where the guitar plays soul/ bluesy licks in between the vocal melody phrases, before ending on the 16th-note figure played over the C^7 chord to finish.

D'Angelo

SONG TITLE: SPANISH JOINT
ALBUM: VOODOO
LABEL: VIRGIN
GENRE: NEO SOUL / R&B / FUNK

WRITTEN BY: D'ANGELO
PRODUCED BY: AND ROY HARGROVE
D'ANGELO

US CHART PEAK: 1

BACKGROUND INFO

'Spanish Joint' is featured on the highly acclaimed *Voodoo* by D'Angelo, released in early 2000. The record is regarded a milestone in the neo-soul genre and inspired a myriad of different artists in the style and beyond. The record won Grammy Awards for Best R&B Album and Best Male R&B Performance.

Voodoo packs in a singular blend of funk, R&B and soul wrapped into a hypnotic and laid-back feel very much D'Angelo's own. This is a critical element in his music and is something he has developed further on each of his releases. D'Angelo's first record, *Brown Sugar*, successfully established this trend in the context of traditional R&B song formats. On *Voodoo*, a much anticipated release after nearly five years, D'Angelo pushed the boundaries of his own writing and produced a layered and at times more abstract set of compositions, paying homage to some of his heroes including Prince, Curtis Mayfield, Miles Davis, and Jimi Hendrix. He composed every part on the record. The J Dilla influenced drum programming and playing adds a unique flavour and atmosphere to the record. The rhythm section work interacts in a highly original and effective way creating a new image of the relaxed feel D'Angelo is credited with developing

A significant influence on 'Spanish Joint' is that of Charlie Hunter, who played eight-string electric guitar, handling guitar and bass simultaneously. His playing adds a singular twist to the feel and atmosphere of the song. Hunter's lead work and bass line are a consummate example of lyrical and complimentary accompaniment. 'Spanish Joint' is a song about karma and was written by D'Angelo and trumpet player Roy Hargrove who is also featured on the record and provided the horn arrangements for the song.

Charlie Hunter is a highly original voice in contemporary guitar playing. He possesses an amazing technical ability but retains a musicality that makes his music accessible to a wide audience. His early influences were Joe Pass and Tuck Andress but he also studied with Joe Satriani. He moved to Paris aged 18 and busked in the city streets for some time, he claims this was a fundamental experience for him. Charlie Hunter has recorded with artists including John Mayer, Dionne Farris, Stanton Moore, Frank Ocean and Snarky Puppy amongst many others.

Spanish Joint

D'Angelo
Words & Music by Angela Stone,
Michael Archer & Roy Hargrove

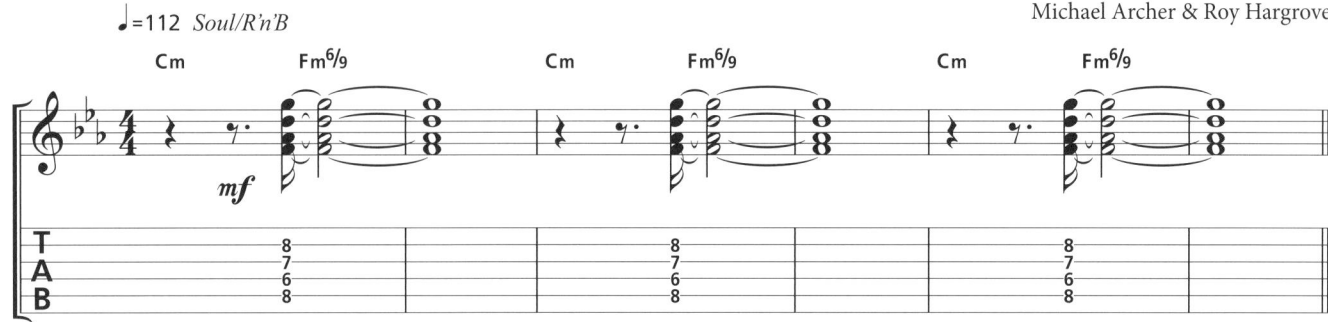

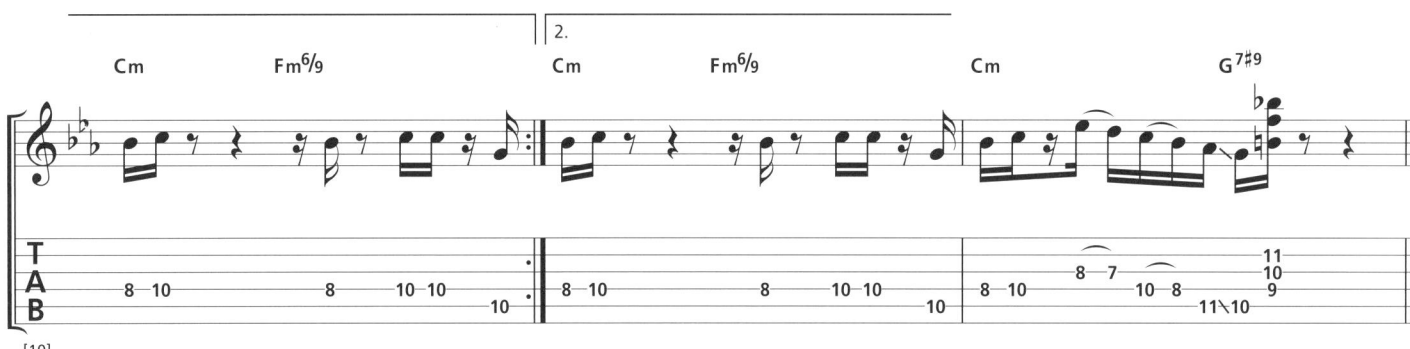

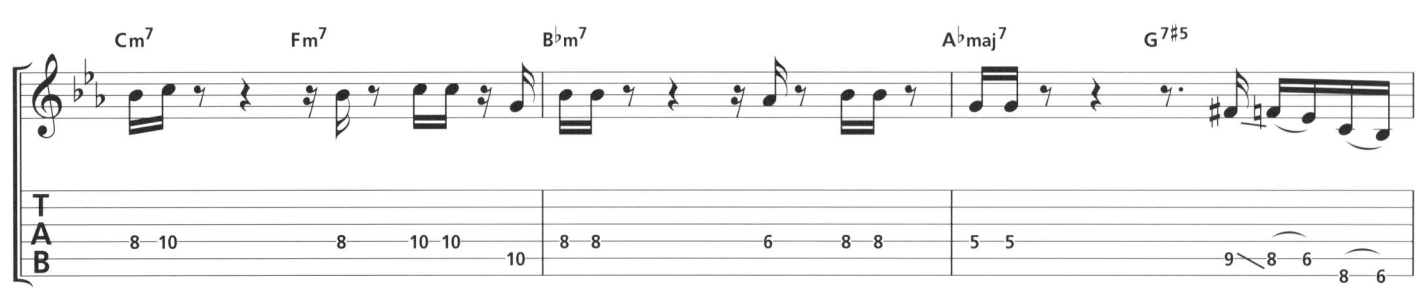

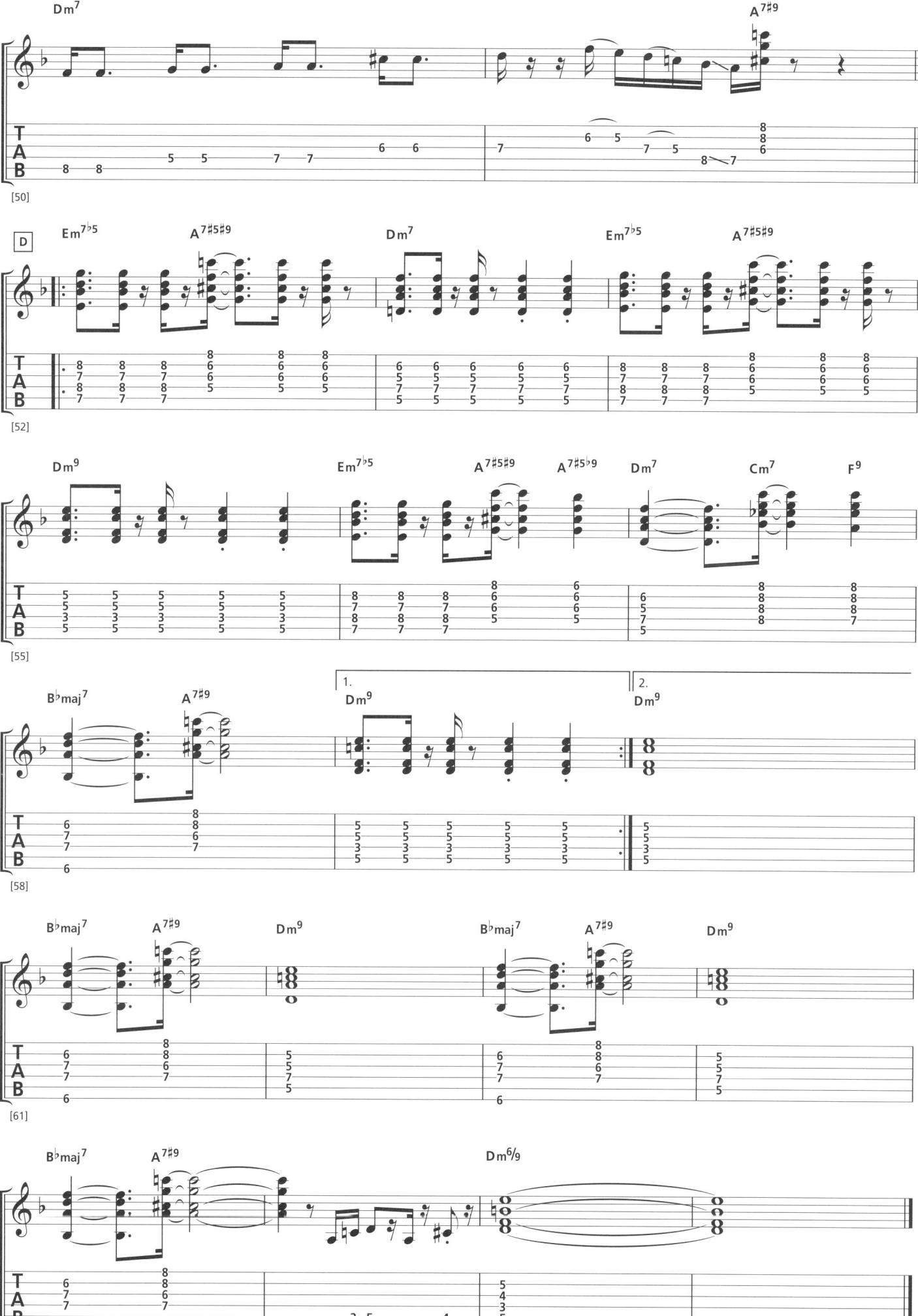

Walkthrough

Amp Settings

For this song a 'warm' clean sound is used throughout. The song was recorded on a guitar fitted with hum-buckers and was set to the neck position.

Note that the EQ levels above are just suggestions. Depending on the guitar and amplifier you play through these settings will change, so it's really important to experiment with pickup selection and tone settings on your guitar to see what different tonal colours you like and feel suit the sound of the song the best.

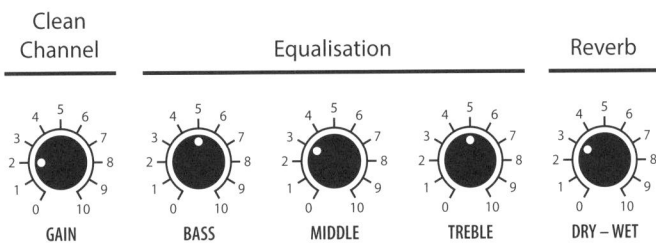

Intro

The song is in the key of C minor and starts with a pentatonic bass line ending on the 4 (F), where the guitar plays an $Fm^{6/9}$ (R, $\flat$3, 6, 9) chord. The guitar then plays a 16th-note minor pentatonic popping line over the main groove to set up the verse section (A). Take note of measure 12 (second time measure) where both bass and guitar play a 16th-note unison line ending on the V chord (G altered).

A Section (Verse)

The A section continues with the 16th-note popping line throughout this section, with variations over the $B\flat m^7$, $A\flat maj^7$ and $G^{7(\sharp5)}$ chords. The section ends with the unison figure over the G altered. Take the repeat back to the beginning of section A.

B Section (Chorus)

The B section (chorus) is based around a minor ii, V, i chord progression: $Dm^{7\flat5}$, G altered and Cm. Watch out for the variation in measure 24 where a Cm^9 is played instead of the Cm^7. Try using a pick, but you may find that the side of your thumb will give you a subtle, consistent tone for these chord changes.

C Section (Solo)

The main challenge with the solo is the 16th-note syncopated feel throughout. The solo is predominantly based around the pentatonic scale, with other intervals to give more 'flavour' to the overall sound. Notice the major 6th and major 9 intervals in the first few phrases of the solo, which hints at the Dorian modal sound.

In measure 40 the chords move through a ii, V, leading to a $A\flat maj^7$ chord ($\flat$vi of Cm) in measure 41. Notice how the use of chromatic intervals are used to 'weave' through the changes here. The preceding chord before the modulation in measure 44 is an $A^{7(\sharp5\sharp9)}$, which is the V chord of the new key D minor. The solo continues in the key of D minor until measure 51 where the solo ends with the unison line ending on the $A^{7(\sharp9)}$ chord.

D Section (Chorus)

The D section (chorus) follows the same form as section B, but now in the new key of Dm. At the second time ending measure (60), the song cycles around the $\flat VI$ ($B\flat maj^7$), V (A altered), then resolving to the tonic (Dm^9). At measure 66 the guitar and bass play a unison figure before ending on a $Dm^{6/9}$ chord in the last measure.

Justin Timberlake

SONG TITLE: CRY ME A RIVER
ALBUM: JUSTIFIED
LABEL: JIVE
GENRE: DISCO/R&B

WRITTEN BY: JUSTIN TIMBERLAKE, TIMOTHY MOSLEY AND SCOTT STORCH
PRODUCED BY: TIMBALAND

US CHART PEAK: 3

BACKGROUND INFO

Justin Timberlake wrote 'Cry Me A River' as a reflection of his breakup with Britney Spears. It is the story of a brokenhearted man who tries to move away from his girlfriend who cheated on him. The song was produced by Timbaland and features vocal and string elements that give the arrangement a haunting nature. 'Cry Me A River' blends various elements of R&B with a lyrical vocal style.

'Cry Me a River' was a massive worldwide success. It peaked at no. 3 on the Billboard Hot 100 chart and the Billboard Top 40. Combined worldwide sales of the single neared three million. The video for the song was also a massive success with nearly 260 million views on YouTube alone.

Timbaland's production lends itself to effective live renditions of the song. Timberlake started playing 'Cry Me A River' live during the *Justified World Tour* in 2003. He continues to perform it to date.

Guitarist and producer Bill Pettaway played on the studio session for 'Cry Me A River'. He is associated with Timbaland with whom he works on a regular basis. His credits include The Lox, SWV ft. Missy Eliott, Total, Ginuwine, Snoop Dogg, Aaliyah, Missy ft. 702, Playa, The Braxtons, Bubba Sparxxx and Milli Vanilli, who's cover of 'Girl You Know It's True' was a huge hit single. Pettaway originally wrote the song for Numarx in 1987. He also recorded 'Justified' for Justin Timberlake.

Justin Timberlake is no stranger to fame having been a cast member in *The Mickey Mouse Club* alongside Britney Spears and Christina Aguilera. The latter would become a tour mate and the former his girlfriend. Timberlake's solo career began after a highly successful stint with boy band NSYNC, he was one of two lead singers together with JC Chasez. His solo career reached even further heights upon the release of his second album *FutureSex/LoveSounds*. Justin Timberlake counts Michael Jackson, Stevie Wonder, Prince, David Bowie, Michael Hutchence and David Byrne amongst his influences.

Justified was awarded a Grammy for Best Pop Vocal Album in 2004 – that is one of ten Grammy awards Justin Timberlake has received to date. Timberlake has sold over 32 million albums as a solo artist, 56 million singles, and 70 million records as a member of NSYNC, making him one of the best-selling artists of all time.

Cry Me A River (live iTunes Festival 2013)

Justin Timberlake
Words & Music by Justin Timberlake, Scott Storch & Tim Mosley

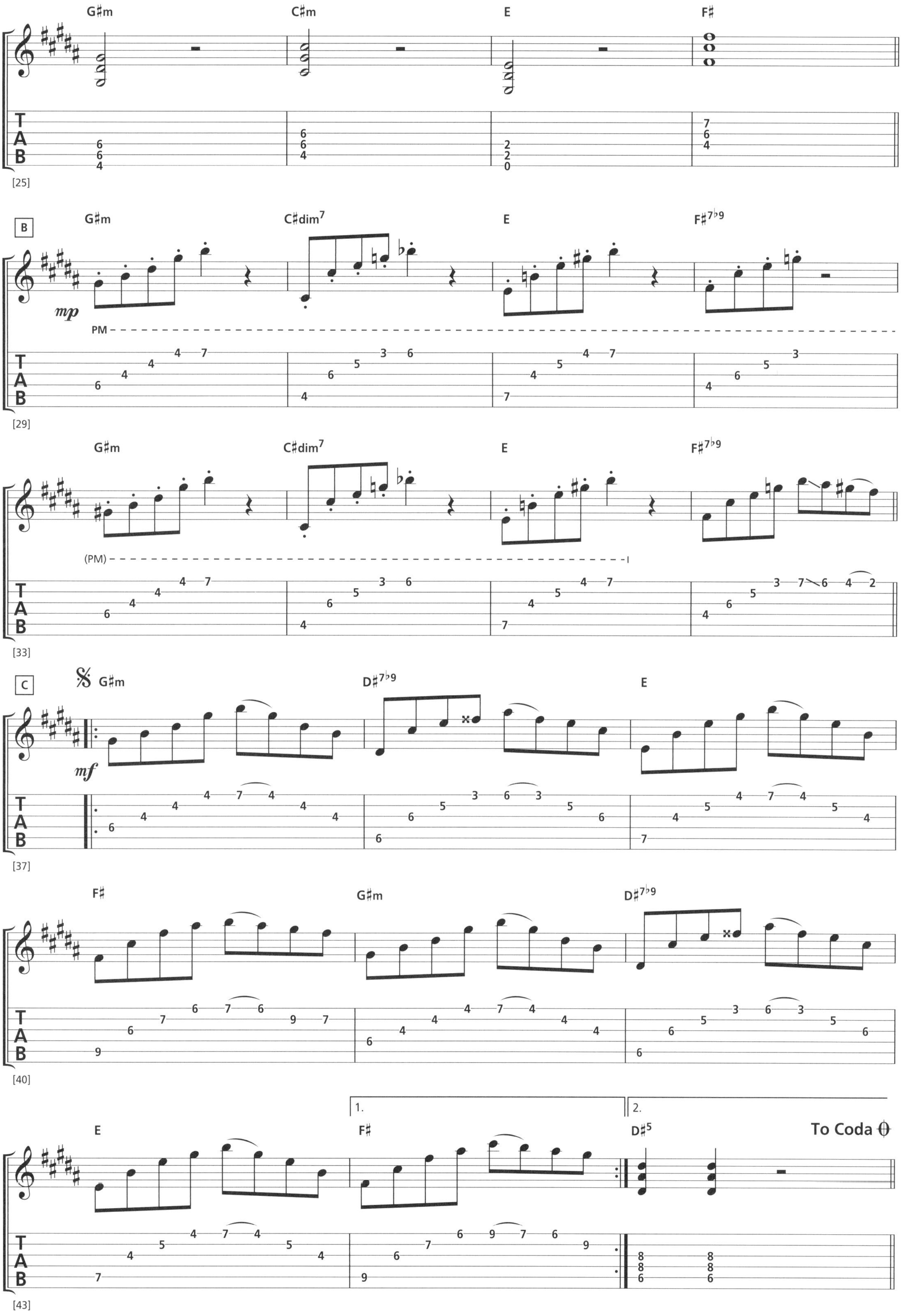

G♯m
C♯m
E
F♯
[25]
B
G♯m
C♯dim7
E
F♯7♭9
mp
PM
[29]
G♯m
C♯dim7
E
F♯7♭9
(PM)
[33]
C
G♯m
D♯7♭9
E
mf
[37]
F♯
G♯m
D♯7♭9
[40]
1.
2.
E
F♯
D♯5
To Coda
[43]

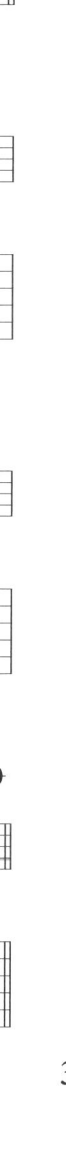

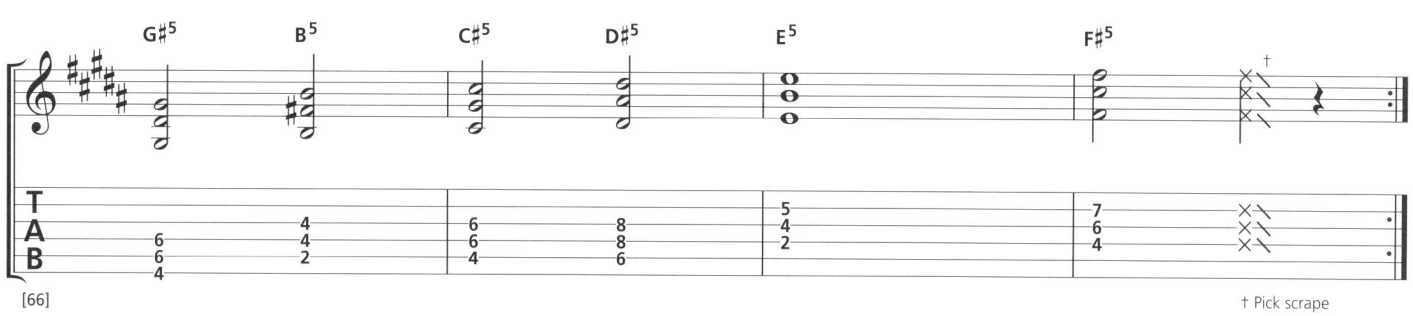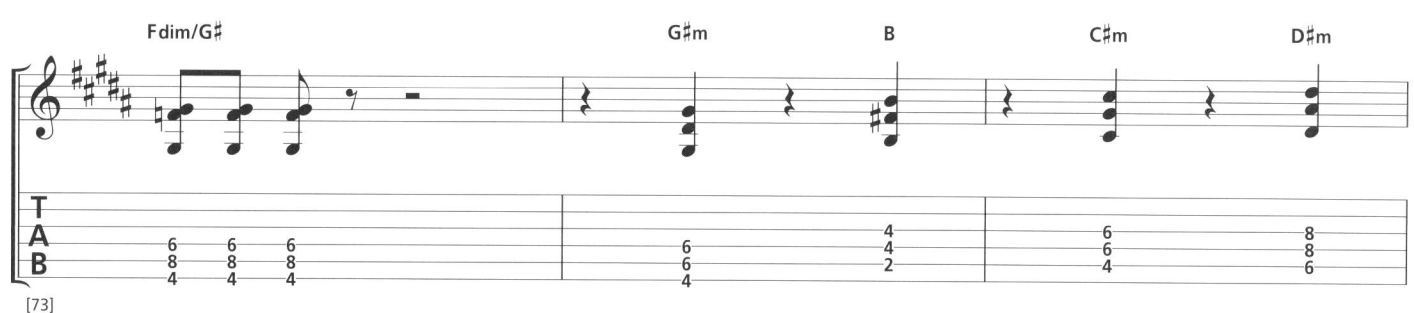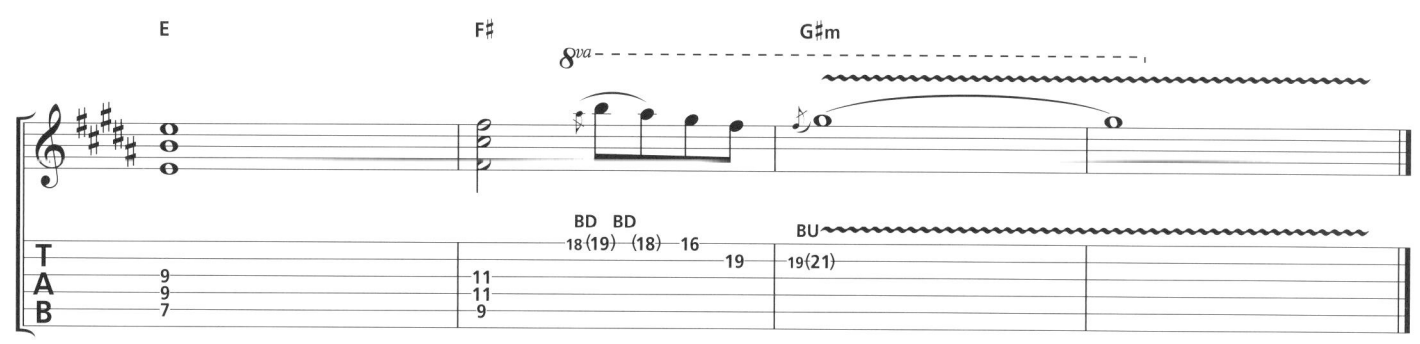

Walkthrough

Amp Settings

The guitar has a distorted tone throughout, and you may want to consider using the volume control to adjust the gain levels between the sections. If you are thinking of using effects in the assessment maybe try using a subtle delay during the solo, or you may want to use a distortion pedal in front of the amp. Note, these settings are just suggestions. Depending on the guitar and amplifier you play through these settings will change! Most importantly, make sure you are happy with your sound!

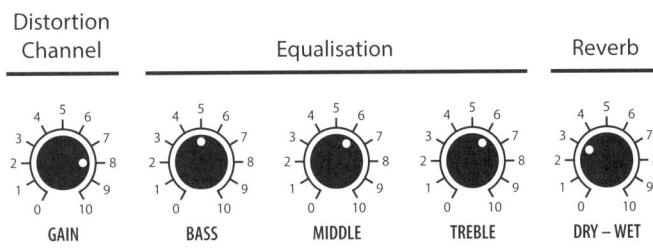

Into and A Section (Verse)

This song is in the key of G♯ minor. The intro starts with the guitar playing arpeggios in unison with the keys following the changes G♯m (i), D♯$^{7♭9}$ (v), E (♭VI), C♯dim^7 (iv dim^7). The C♯dim^7 chord is an inversion of the leading chord in the G♯ harmonic minor scale, F𝄪dim^7 (F double-sharp dim^7). Watch out for the F double-sharps throughout the song. The use of palm muting will help keep the notes short, and not too intrusive to the overall sound. From measure 9 to measure 12 bass and drums enter, with the guitar playing power chords creating a dynamic shift setting up the beginning of the A section. The guitar in the A section plays half note power chords on beat 1 of each measure, with unison fills played with the bass in measures 16 and 24. Watch out for the stops in measures 20, 21 and 22.

B Section (Bridge)

In the B section the guitar returns to playing arpeggios over the changes, G♯m (i), C♯dim^7 (iv dim^7), E (♭VI) and F♯$^{7♭9}$ (♭VII), leading into the C section. Notice the last measure in this section is to be played without Palm muting, as a dynamic 'ramp' into the C section.

C Section (Solo)

The solo is based around the G natural minor scale, with a 'nod' to G harmonic minor in the last measure (60). The main challenges with this solo are the eighth note triplet feel in measure 49, which may feel like a finger twister to begin with. Apart from the first pull off on beat 1, the whole lick is alternate picked, but you may find 'sweep picking' the last triplet (G♯ min triad) an easier way to transition into the bend on beat 1 of measure 50. As the solo is played in the 'upper' register of the guitar, it's best to work on intonation of the bends and general articulation, as it can become 'fiddly' as the frets get smaller! After the solo take the ***D.S.*** back to the sign at section C (chorus) until you get to the ***To Coda*** sign at measure 62.

D Section

At section D the band launches into a half time groove reminiscent of a certain rock band of the 70s. Spend some time becoming comfortable with the chord voicing in this section, and the rhythmic variations of the unison stabs from measure 70. The song ends with a guitar and bass unison line finishing with a long held G♯ bend.

Albert Lee

SONG TITLE: COUNTRY BOY
ALBUM: HEADS HANDS & FEET
LABEL: SEE FOR MILES RECORDS
GENRE: BLUES ROCK / COUNTRY / BLUEGRASS / FOLK

WRITTEN BY: ALBERT LEE
PRODUCED BY: HEADS HANDS & FEET

US COUNTRY
CHART PEAK: 1

BACKGROUND INFO

Albert Lee's guitar playing is so fluid, lyrical and distinguishable that he is in a class all of his own. He wrote 'Country Boy' whilst a member of Heads Hands & Feet, a combo that featured Pete Gavin on drums, Tony Colton on vocals, Ray Smith on guitar, Chas Hodges on bass, violin and vocals and Mike O'Neill on keyboards. In 1973 the band splintered and Albert Lee formed his own band with Pete Gavin and Chas Hodges who would later form the duo Chas & Dave with Dave Peacock.

'Country Boy' features a number of lightning fast solo breaks displaying Lee's phenomenal musicality and impeccable technique. His finger style and hybrid picking are of the highest order. Albert Lee relocated to Los Angeles in 1974 having spent all his life in the UK where he grew up amongst pioneers of the guitar such as Eric Clapton, Jeff Beck, Ritchie Blackmore and Jimmy Page with whom he swapped place in bands on a number of occasions.

In 1971 he recorded Jon Lord's *Gemini Suite*. Upon arriving in Los Angeles he recorded with The Crickets and did extensive session work. In 1976 he was asked to join Emmylou Harris's Hot Band in which he replaced James Burton, one of his heroes, who was returning to play in Elvis Presley's band. Amongst those featured in Emmylou Harris' Hot Band was Ricky Skaggs who recorded 'Country Boy' in 1985 topping the country charts in the US.

In 1978 Albert Lee joined Eric Clapton's band – his stay lasted five years and he recorded a memorable live solo on 'Cocaine', featured on *Just One Night*. Albert Lee defined much of the sound of the Fender Telecaster but later started playing Music Man guitars, who would go on to build his signature model. Some of his guitars are fitted with a B-Bender, an integral part of Lee's sound.

In 1983 Lee was responsible for the Everly Brothers' Reunion Concert and was its musical director. He played regularly with the Everly Brothers for over twenty years.

Albert Lee won a Grammy Award in 2002 for his contribution on 'Foggy Mountain Breakdown'. Lee's discography as sideman and band leader includes over 100 titles. He is highly respected by fellow musicians for his humble and self-effacing personality and his enormous musical gift.

Country Boy

Albert Lee
Words & Music by Albert Lee,
Tony Colton & Raymond Smith

♩=240 *Fast Country*

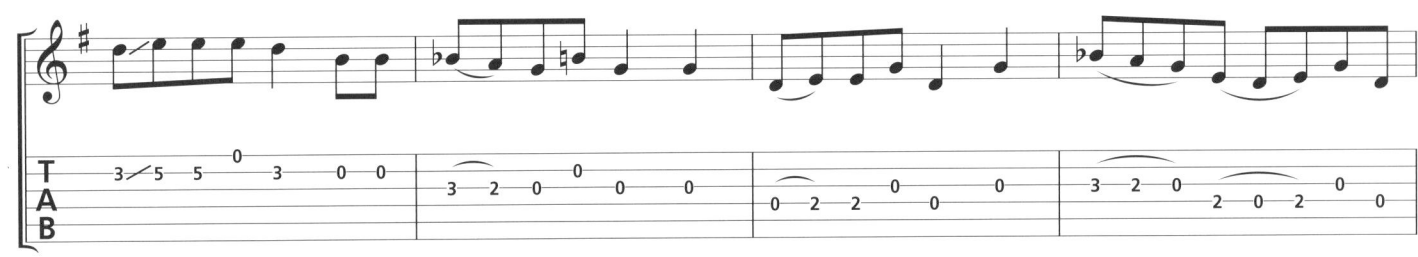

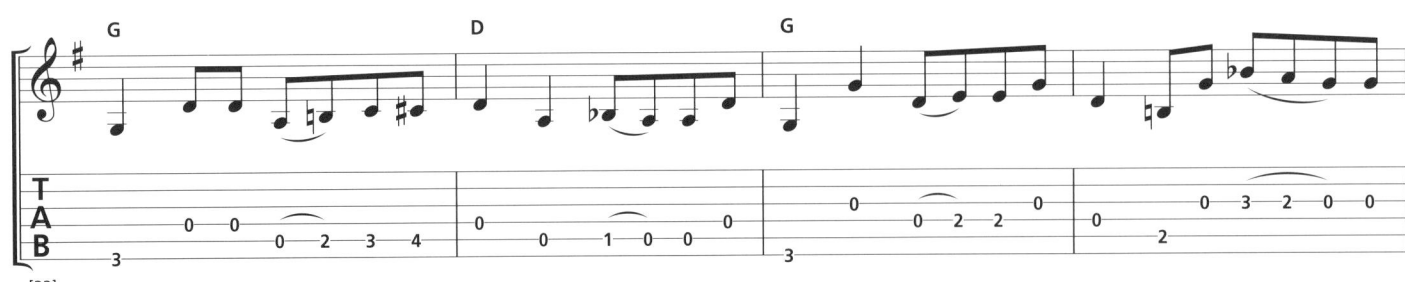

© Copyright 1971 Jamarnie Music Limited.
Universal/Island Music Limited.
All Rights Reserved. International Copyright Secured.

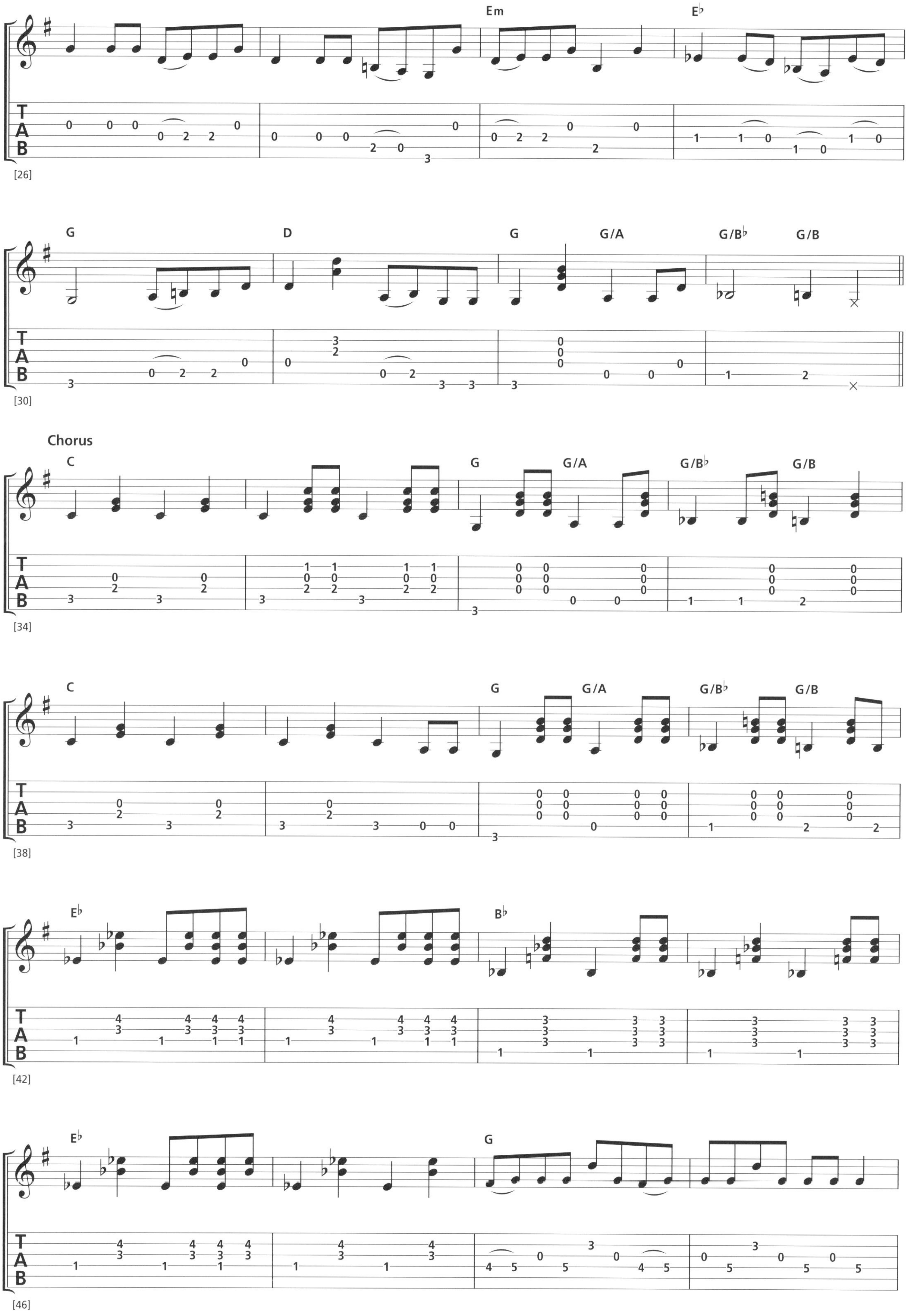
Em
E♭
[26]
G
D
G
G/A
G/B♭
G/B
[30]
Chorus
C
G
G/A
G/B♭
G/B
[34]
C
G
G/A
G/B♭
G/B
[38]
E♭
B♭
[42]
E♭
G
[46]

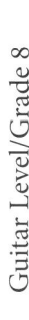

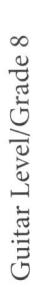

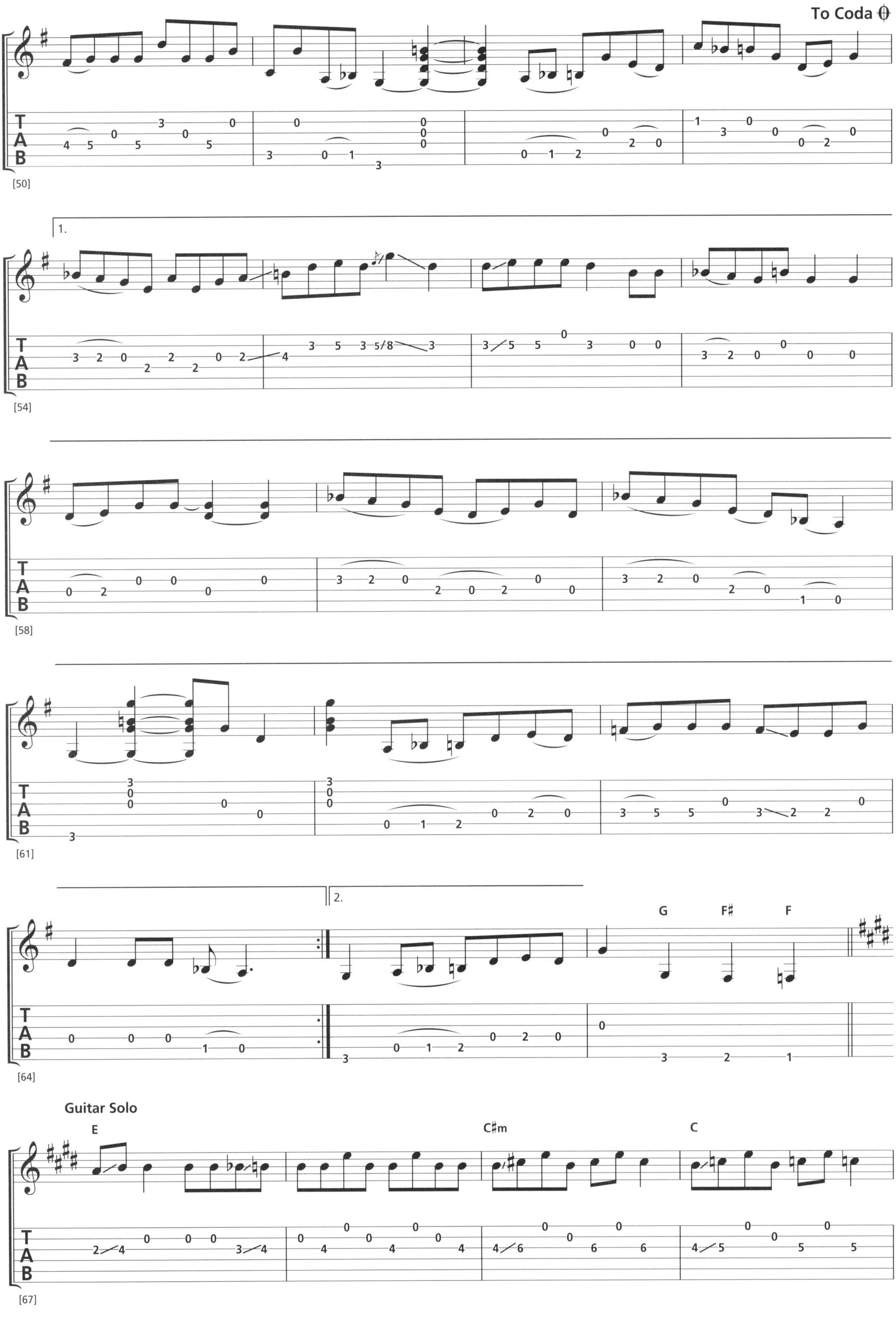
To Coda
[50]
1.
[54]
[58]
[61]
2.
G
F♯
F
[64]
Guitar Solo
E
C♯m
C
[67]

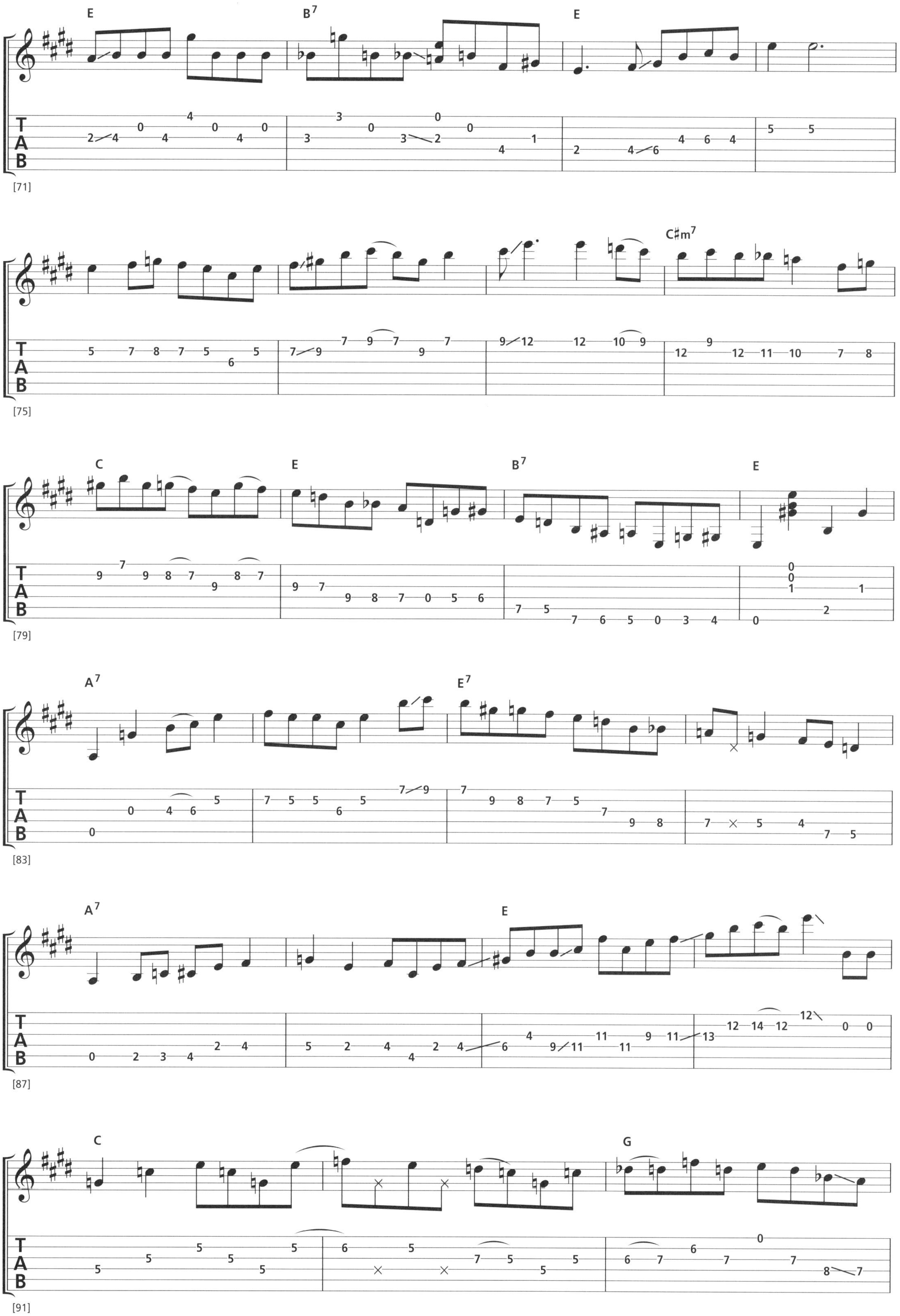
E
B7
E
[71]
C♯m7
[75]
C
E
B7
E
[79]
A7
E7
[83]
A7
E
[87]
C
G
[91]

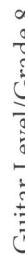

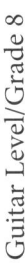

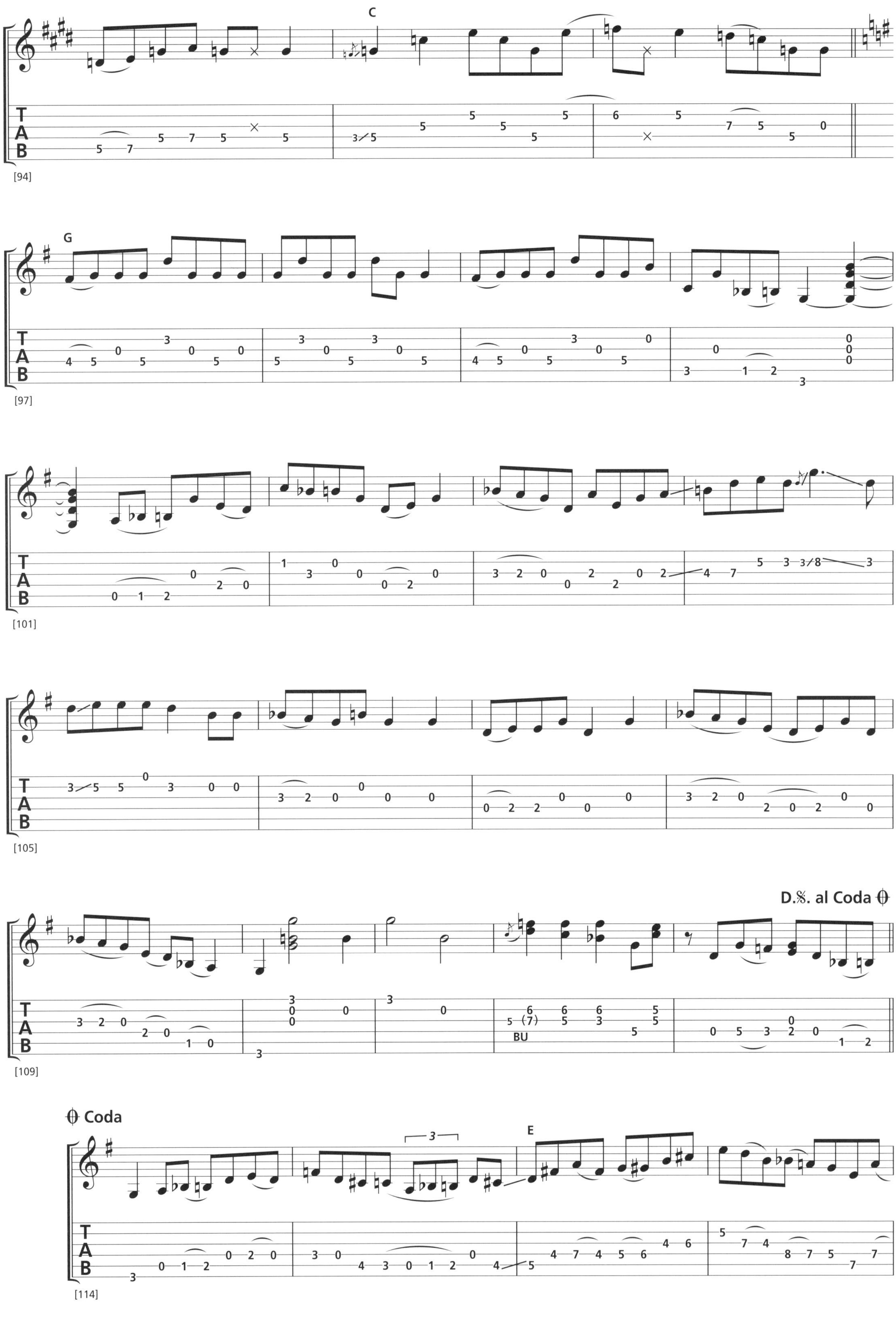
C
[94]
G
[97]
[101]
[105]
D.S. al Coda
BU
[109]
Coda
3
E
[114]

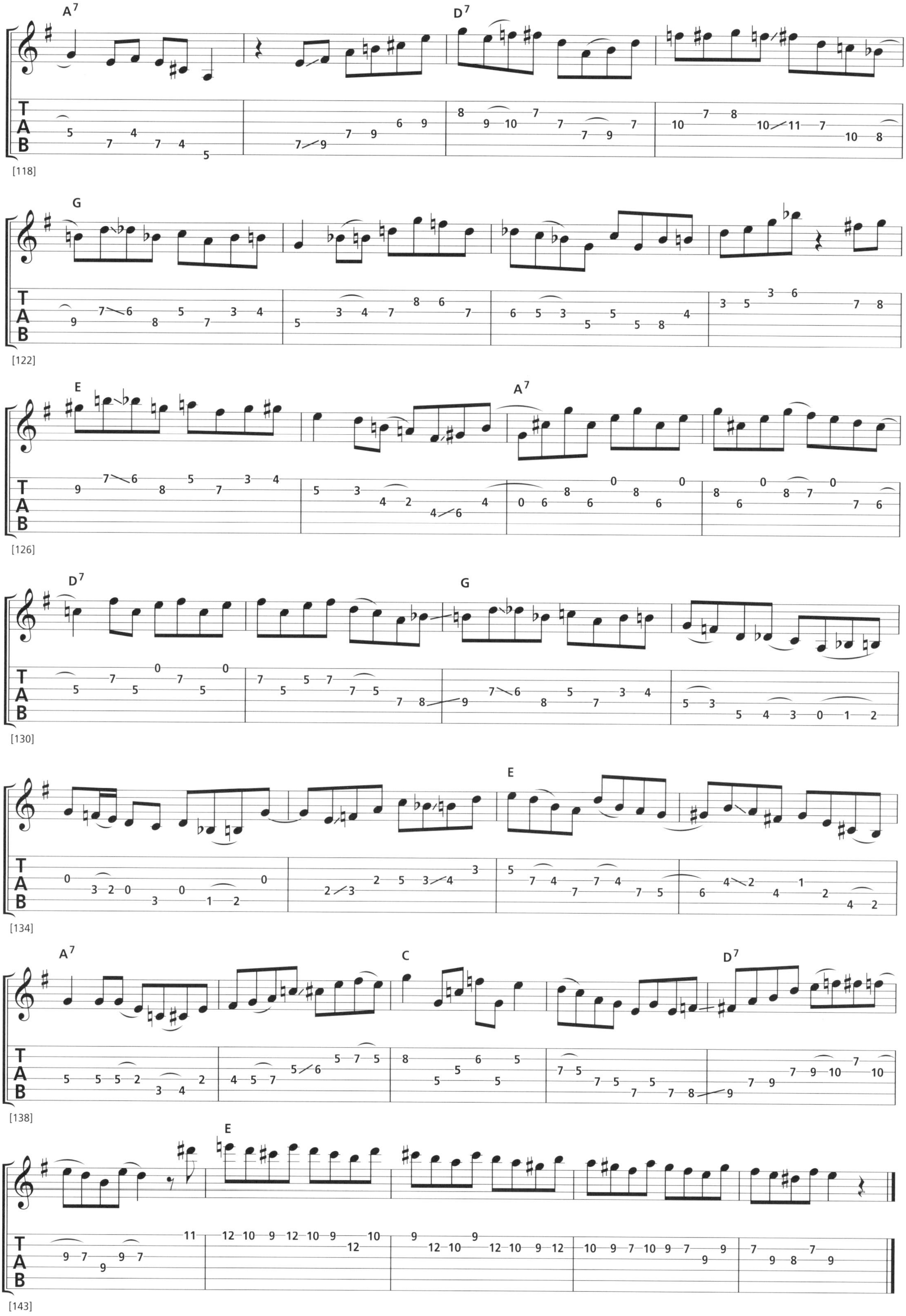
A7
D7
[118]
G
[122]
E
A7
[126]
D7
G
[130]
E
[134]
A7
C
D7
[138]
E
[143]

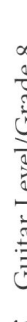

Walkthrough

Amp Settings

Use a classic American style amp with a totally clean sound. Albert uses reverb and often chorus. His use of delay is an important part of his approach.

We chose not to use his signature take on the delay effect here as it would require all students to possess and master the delay effect. This means setting the delay pedal to sound a note 3/16ths of a beat later. The result of this is that playing eighth notes ends up sounding 16th notes by filling the gaps with repeats.

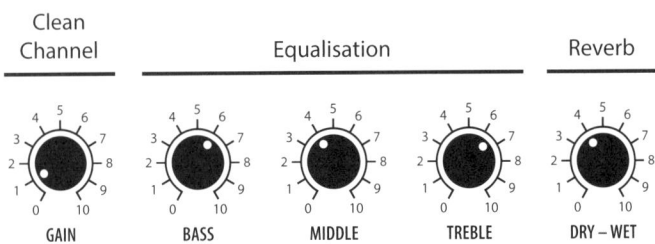

Intro Section (Measures 1–2)

The first thing to note is that Albert uses hybrid picking. This is where a flatpick is used but the middle and ring fingers of the right hand are also employed. This means that patterns which would be impossible to cleanly articulate with a pick become possible. For the first pattern the pick plays the fourth string, the middle finger takes the third string, and the ring finger takes the second string. The use of open strings is an important part of country guitar playing.

Measure 5 is probably the most famous lick in country music – so famous that it is sometimes referred to as 'the lick'. The line moves up chromatically from the 9th to the 3rd. The 6th degree E is also a staple of this approach.

Measure 6 and 7 feature another key part of this style. The major 3rd is approached from a semitone below and in the next measure the minor 3rd is featured – this adds something of a blues character. The use of the open E in measure 9 is also very typical of this style.

First Verse (Measures 18–33)

In this section Albert uses single notes to fill around the chord tones under a vocal line. Measure 18 is a good example. Here the G arpeggio is filled out simply by adding the note A.

Chorus (Measures 34–47)

Here Albert is playing a bass note on beats 1 and 3 with partial chord voicings on the other beats. In other tunes he has often played the root and the 5th as the bass notes, but here he generally just plays the root.

First Solo Section (Measures 67–96)

This is an iconic solo that has influenced countless country guitar players on both sides of the Atlantic.

In measures 67–72, hybrid-picked open strings are used. This is a 'banjo roll' – a standard banjo technique – the pick should take the third string, the middle finger should take the second string, and the ring finger should play the top string. The lick in measure 72 is fantastic and is well worth incorporating into your improvising on other tunes.

Measure 75–76 is an interesting lick. The underlying chord is E. In the first measure Albert hits a bluesy G natural, in the second he states the major 3rd really strongly and adds the colourful 6th degree. This is a perfect demonstration that Albert is one of those players where it will be worth analysing the function of the notes he plays against the chords. There's a reason why he's still revered amongst guitarists.

Second Solo Section (Measures 114–147)

The first two measures of this solo are a classic modern country idea. This approach has been absorbed by Brent Mason and Brad Paisley.

Measure 115 starts with the flat 7th followed by three notes that lead chromatically down from D to C. Just as you think we're running down chromatically to the 3rd degree B, we jump down and approach the B chromatically up from A. This is a technique that jazz musicians call enclosure – and this is an advanced use of the idea.

Measure 116 uses a D triad, then approaches the major third of the E chord from the bluesy minor third, before employing the jazzy sounding 6th.

Meet Darth Ear

SONG TITLE: MEET DARTH EAR
GENRE: PROGRESSIVE METAL
TEMPO: 120 BPM
KEY: E MINOR

TECH FEATURES: ALTERNATE PICKING
SYNCOPATED RIFFS
TIME SIGNATURE CHANGES

COMPOSERS: CHARLIE GRIFFITHS
& JASON BOWLD

PERSONNEL: CHARLIE GRIFFITHS (GTR)
DAVE MARKS (BASS)
JASON BOWLD (DRUMS)

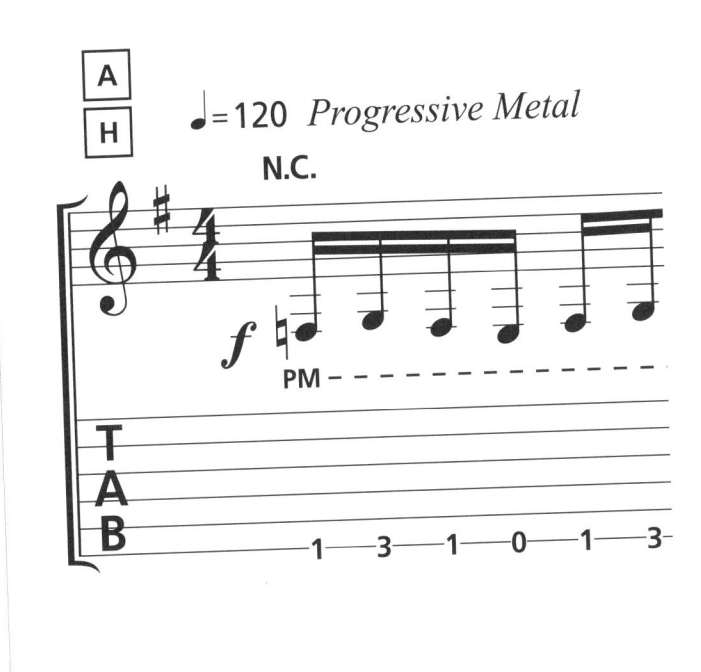

OVERVIEW

'Meet Darth Ear' is a progressive metal track in the style of bands like Dream Theater, Periphery and Symphony X. It begins with an alternate picked 16th note riff followed by a crunchy E phrygian section that features numerous odd time changes. The melodic verse uses extended arpeggios based in E natural minor. This is a challenging section to play cleanly because there are lots of string changes and position shifts. The chorus comprises of ringing sustained chords that provide some respite before the solo, which is played over a similar natural minor based progression to that of the verse.

STYLE FOCUS

Progressive metal features heavy, technical riffs that are usually played with a tone and intensity comparable to those of thrash metal but with more complex rhythms and lots of time signature changes. The style demands technical excellence and precision in all metal based techniques but relies mainly on alternate picking and legato. Prog metal compositions are often long and contain various dynamic shifts. It's common for lead guitar parts to switch between modes: lydian, phrygian, harmonic minor and melodic minor are the most frequently used.

THE BIGGER PICTURE

Prog metal emerged in the late 1980s when Queensrÿche, Fates Warning and other metal bands were influenced by the cerebral approach of 1970s prog rock bands like Yes, Rush and King Crimson. In 1992, a group of ex-Berklee College of Music students named Dream Theater refined this concept and released *Images And Words* (1992), an album with a level of musicianship never heard before in metal. John Petrucci displayed guitar chops to match the likes of Steve Vai, while the complex song structures and highly arranged unison passages were unrivalled. Today Dream Theater continue to dominate the genre. However, bands like Tool, Porcupine Tree and Opeth have diversified the sound considerably.

RECOMMENDED LISTENING

Queensrÿche's conceptual masterpiece *Operation: Mindcrime* (1988) is a must. Its cinematic feel and Chris DeGarmo's imaginative guitar parts were a big influence on prog metal pioneers Fates Warning, who hit their stride in 1991 with their breakthrough album *Parallels*. Dream Theater released the masterpiece *Images And Words* a year later and *Awake* in 1994. More recently, Pain of Salvation's album *Remedy Lane* (2002) has become a modern classic.

Meet Darth Ear

Charlie Griffiths & Jason Bowld

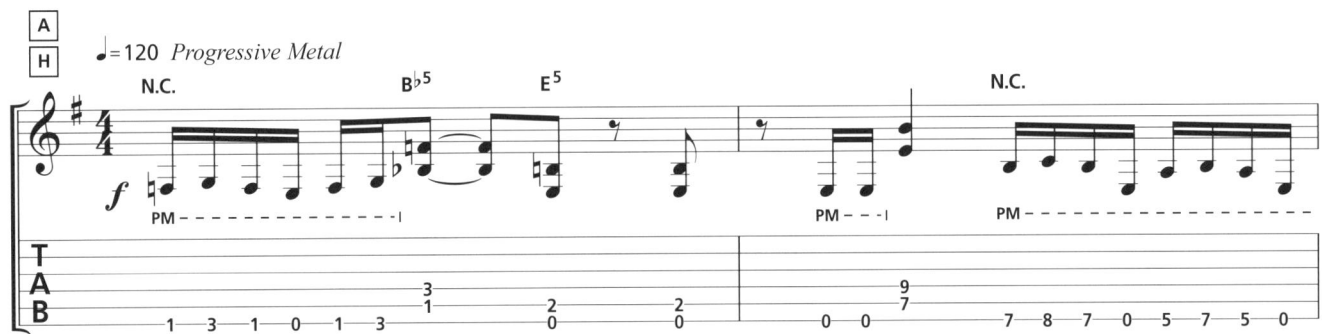
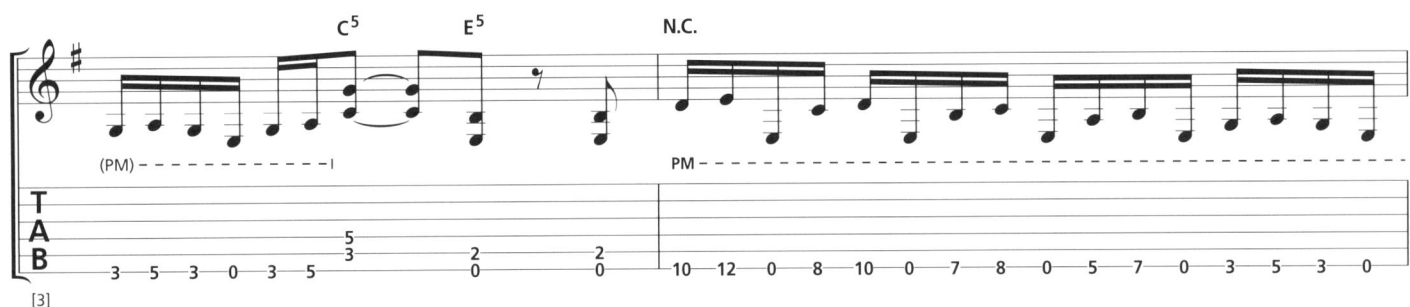
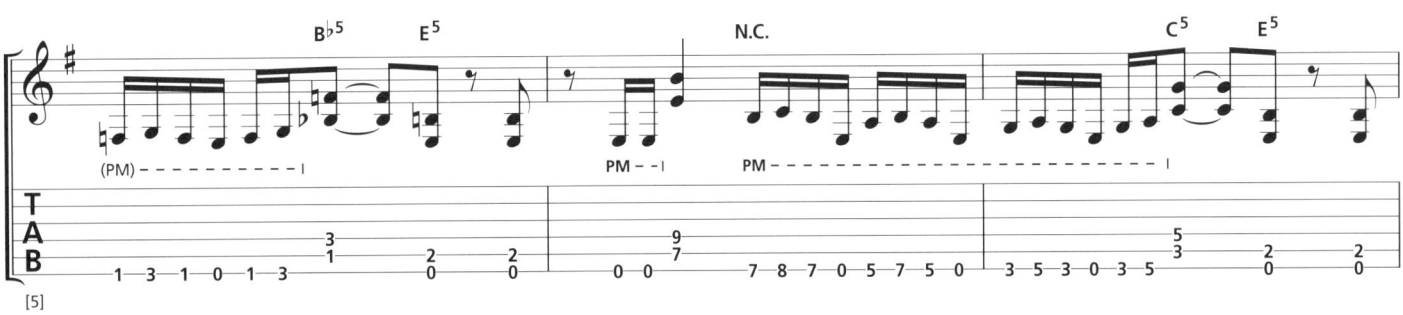

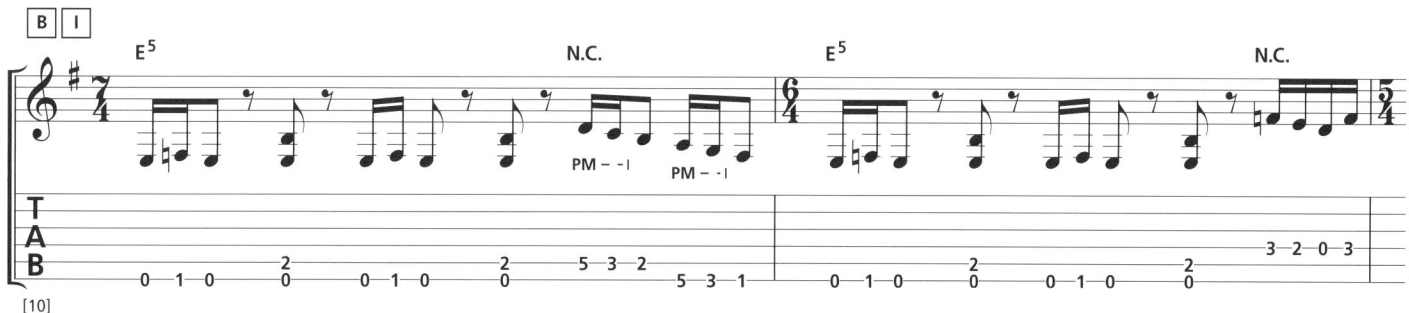
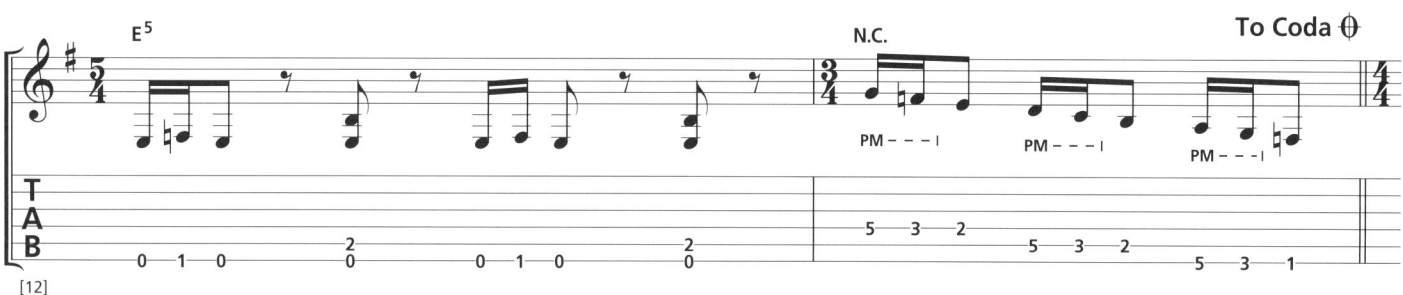
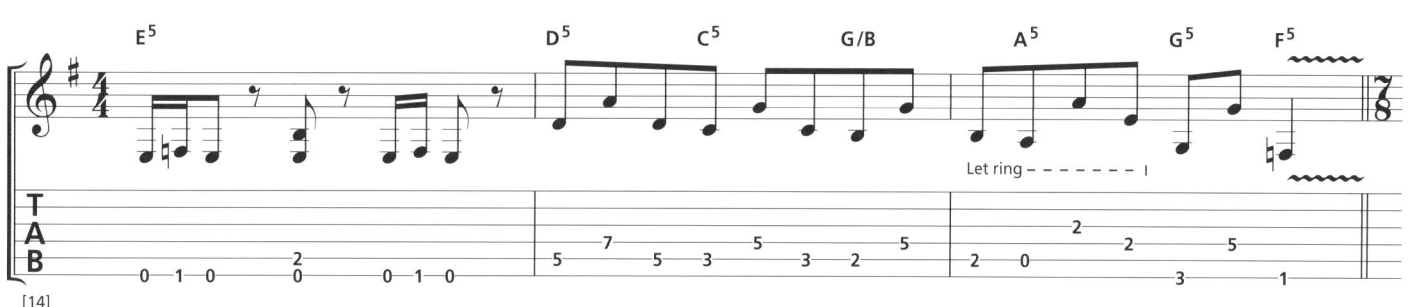

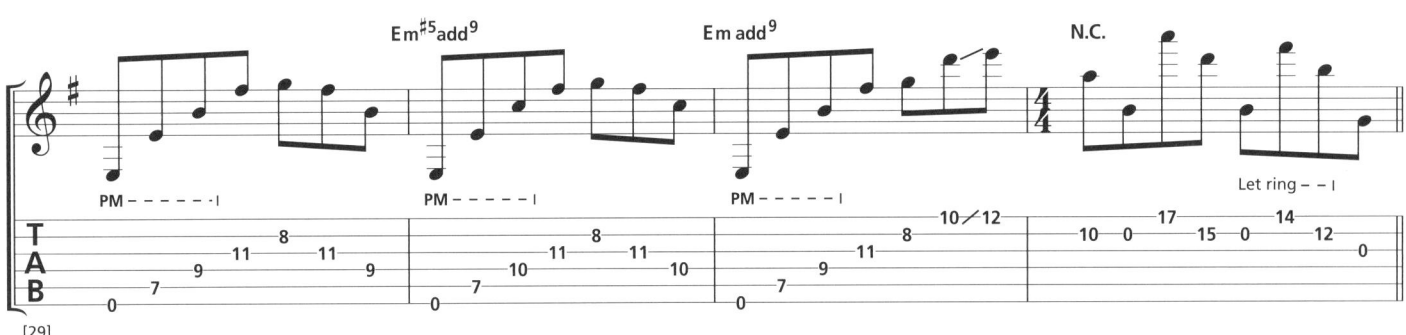

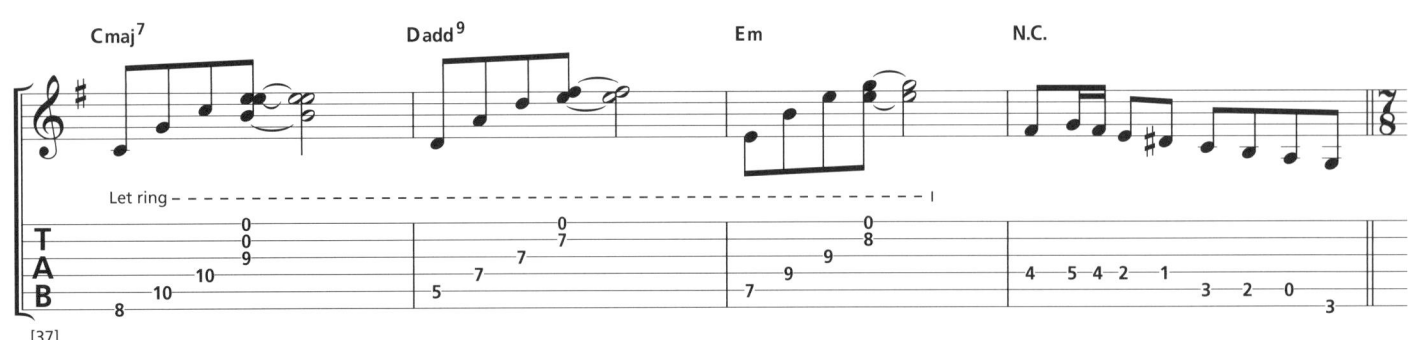

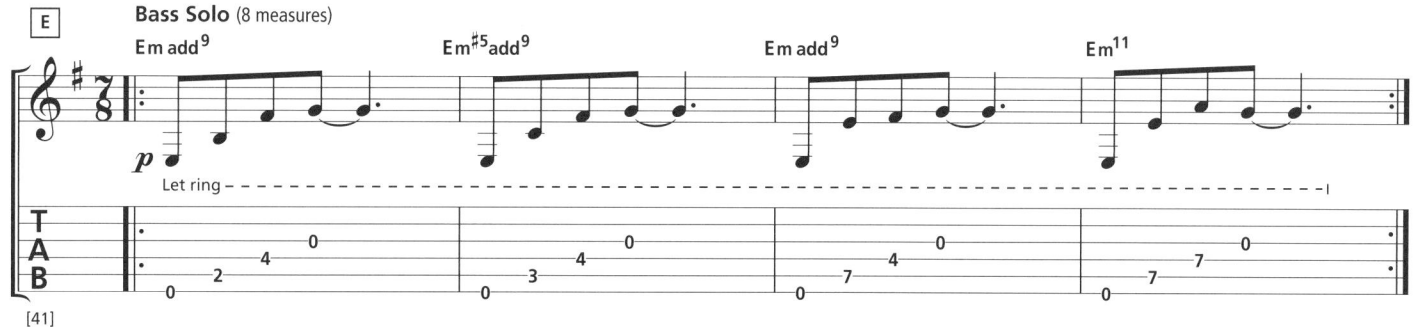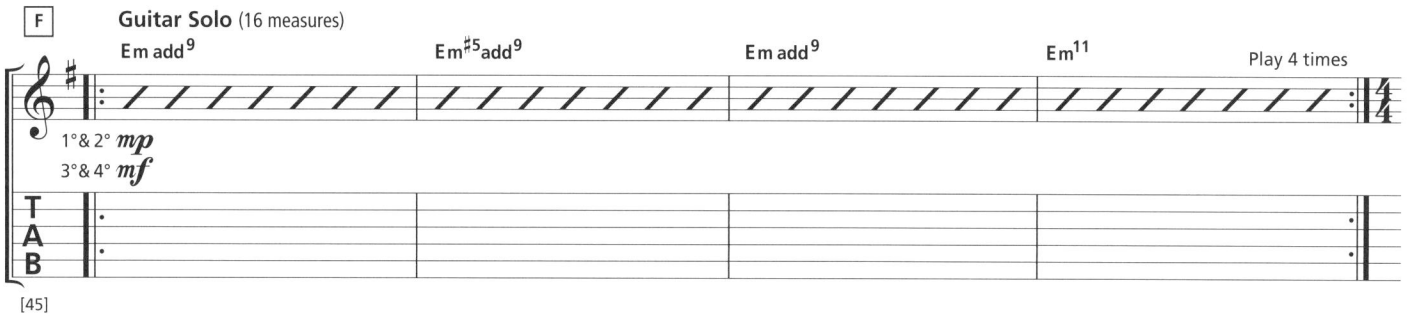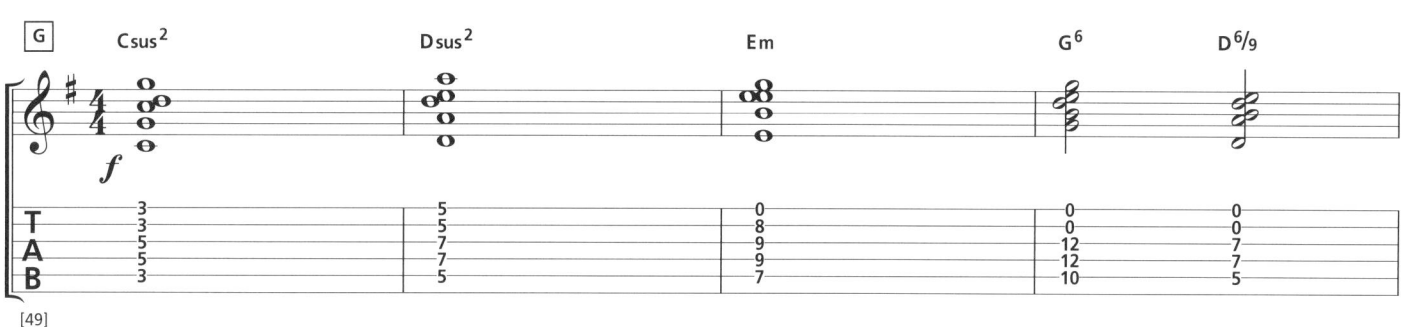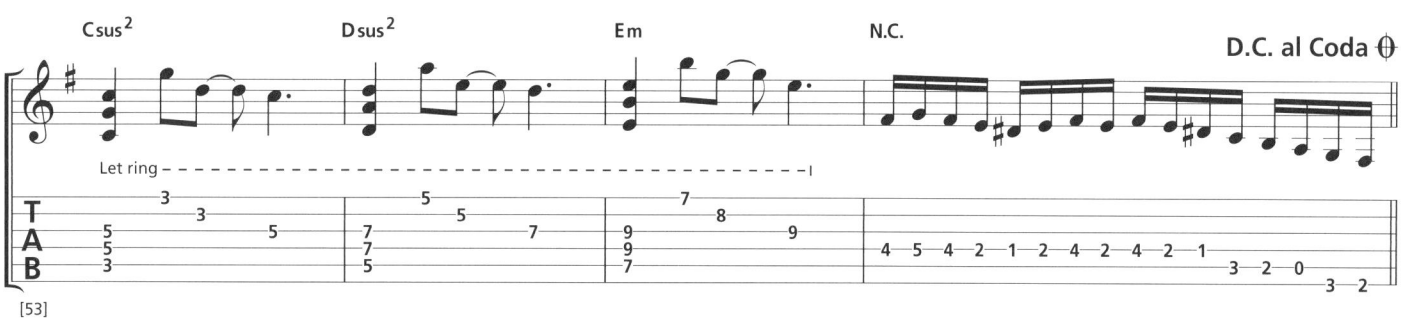

Walkthrough

Amp Settings

The traditional scooped metal tone will work for most of 'Meet Darth Ear' but you may wish to switch to a sound with more middle for the solo. Metal rhythm tones are usually dry (without effects), but it's common to add delay in more melodic sections and solos.

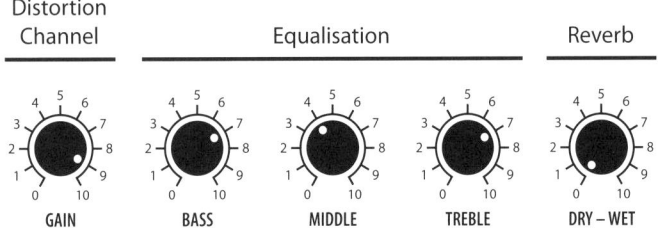

A & H Sections (Measures 1–9)

This section consists of a heavy riff that combines powerchords with low string palm-muted single-note runs that use the E string as a pedal tone.

Measures 1–9 | *Fast picking*
Many of the riffs in 'Meet Darth Ear' feature fast alternate picking, often with palm muting, and will probably take some preparation to play well. Use a relaxed picking action and minimise excess motion where possible: your pick should only travel a small amount past the string. Work on these phrases with the metronome set to a lower speed and only increase it when you can play the part accurately.

B & I Sections (Measures 10–16)

This section is a variation of the opening riff that uses different time signatures.

Measures 10–13 | *Odd time signatures*
If you look closely at these measures you will see that they are based on a five beat riff (Fig. 1). The 7/4 measure is this riff followed by a two-beat phrase. The 6/4 measure is this pattern followed by a one-beat phrase and measure 12 is the five-beat riff on its own followed by a three-beat phrase in measure 13.

C Section (Measures 17–32)

In the C section, the time signature changes to 7/8 and the guitar arpeggiates exotic sounding chords.

Measures 17–31 | *7/8 time signature*
The 7/8 time signature is usually counted as a group of four beats followed by a group of three beats ("1 2 3 4 1 2 3"). If you count along with the music as you are playing, you will find that this time signature has a unique groove which you should be able to lock into and feel naturally.

D & E Sections (Measures 33–44)

The D section is a melodic part that uses chords such as the sus^2 and add^9 to create an open sound. The E section is the bass solo where the time signature returns to 7/8.

Measures 33–44 | *Combining fretted notes with open strings*
Take time to ensure that you play the fretted notes with the tips of your fingers so that the open strings can ring freely.

F & G Sections (Measures 45–56)

The F section is the guitar solo and changes dynamic halfway through. The F section is a frenetic drum solo. Although the guitar plays a simple part, full concentration will be required to maintain the pulse.

Measures 45–48 | *Guitar solo*
The biggest challenge of this solo is playing convincingly in 7/8 time. Start by counting through the measure ("1 2 3 4 1 2 3") playing a note on every beat (Fig. 2). Accent the first beat of each measure to help you feel where the start of each measure is. Once you feel comfortable, play phrases that are more rhythmically interesting but maintain the accent on beat 1 to remind you of the groove. Once you feel you are improvising fluently you should find that you do not have to keep the beat 1 accent.

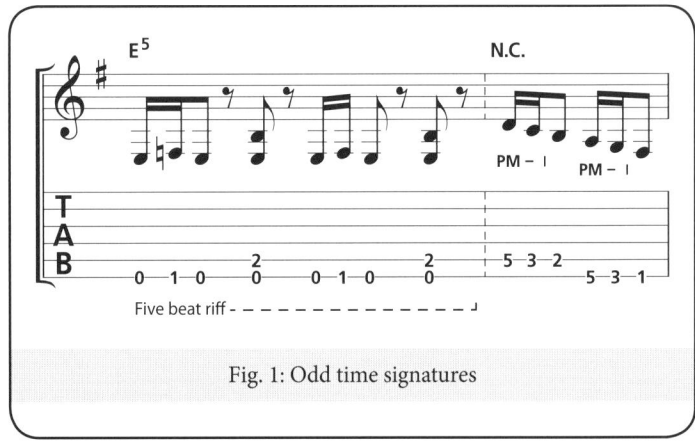

Fig. 1: Odd time signatures

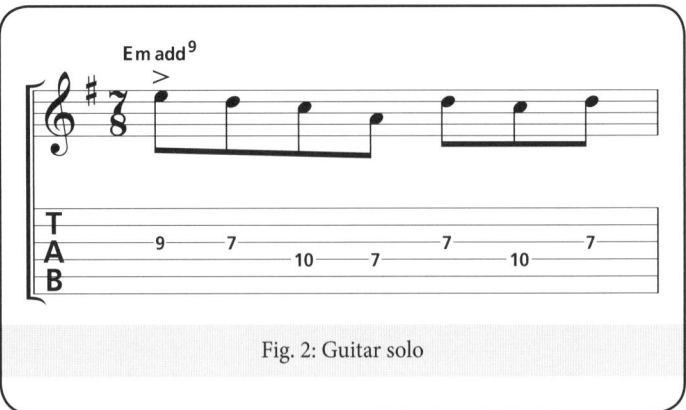

Fig. 2: Guitar solo

Mind The Gaps

SONG TITLE: MIND THE GAPS
GENRE: FUNK
TEMPO: 96 BPM
KEY: Bb

TECH FEATURES: MUTED 16TH NOTE RHYTHMS
ALTERED CHORDS

COMPOSER: KIT MORGAN

PERSONNEL: LARRY CARLTON (GTR)
HENRY THOMAS (BASS)
NOAM LEDERMAN (DRUMS)
FERGUS GERRAND (PERC)
ROSS STANLEY (KEYS)
FULL FAT HORNS (BRASS)

OVERVIEW

'Mind The Gaps' is a funk track in the style of Average White Band, The Crusaders and Tower Of Power. It features triads, altered chords – and a special guest appearance by fusion legend Larry Carlton.

STYLE FOCUS

This piece will test your ability to hold down a tight funk chord part and solo over a complex chord progression. In this type of instrumental funk track the guitar is often at the fore playing melody lines and using more sophisticated and unusual chord voicings. There are also situations where the guitar is the only instrument playing chords so an advanced chord vocabulary is essential, especially if you are to create an interesting harmonic backdrop for a soloist.

THE BIGGER PICTURE

In the 1970s, black music styles merged as jazz musicians achieved commercial success via the popular rhythmic appeal of funk and soul. Groups like Tower Of Power, The Crusaders and Average White Band were able to draw on their knowledge of jazz harmony to create a more complex form of funky soul music that didn't rely as heavily on one-chord vamps as much as James Brown's funk did.

There were those, however, who admired funk's rough edges as much as its rhythmic pull. Miles Davis and Herbie Hancock were established on the jazz scene when Brown created funk in the late 1960s. Both were seduced by its earthiness and wondered how their own improvised music might sound with a stable harmonic base, the complex chords and quick changes of bebop discarded completely. Davis' *Bitches Brew* (1970) and Hancock's *Headhunters* (1973) provided the answer; two wild jazz funk albums of a different nature to their slick contemporaries.

Donald Byrd and his protégés The Blackbyrds occupied the middle ground. The Blackbyrds' eponymous debut (1974) swung from heavy James Brown style funk grooves to jazzy soul improvisations.

RECOMMENDED LISTENING

Tower Of Power's eponymous release of 1973 features their funkiest track, 'What Is Hip?', while Average White Band's 'Pick Up The Pieces' has instrumental funk chord voicings and a catchy rhythm part. Finally, for smooth jazz listen to 'Room 335' from Larry Carlton's self-titled 1978 album.

Mind The Gaps

Kit Morgan

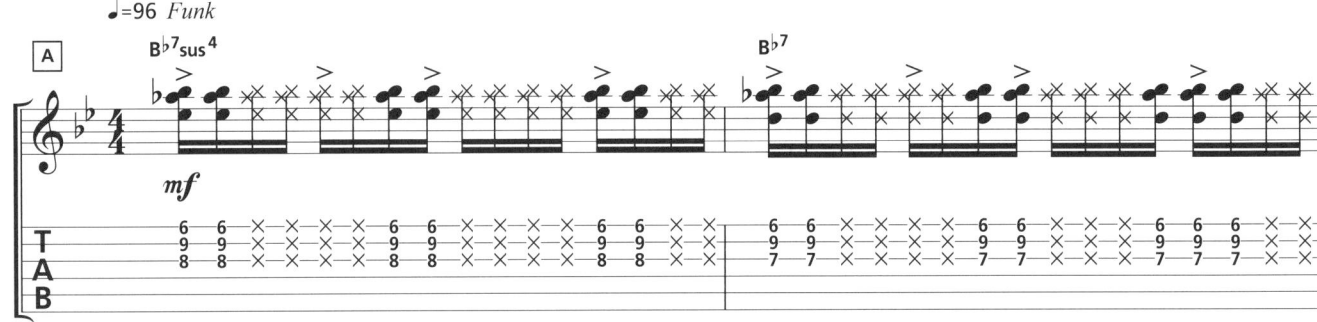
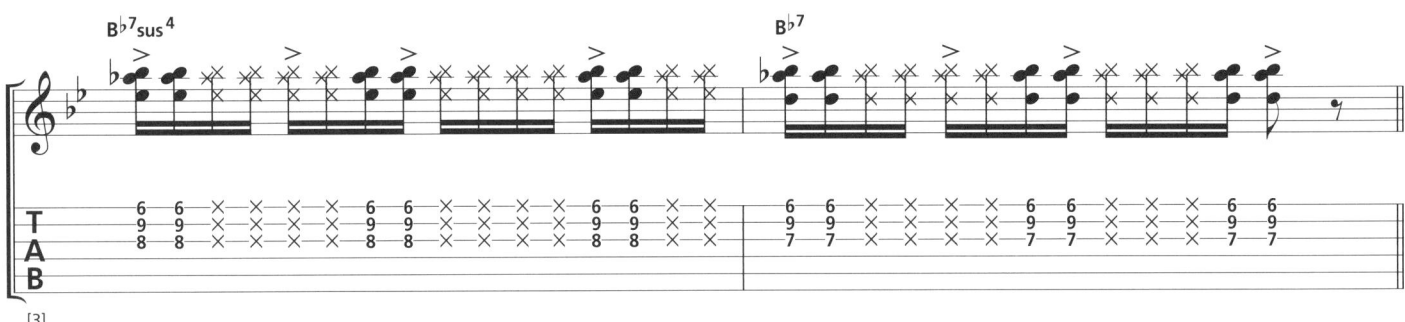
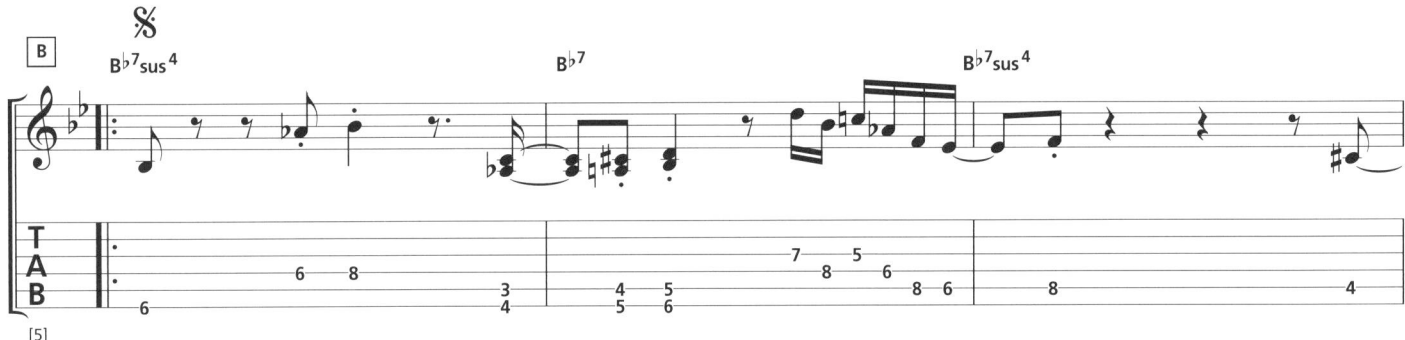

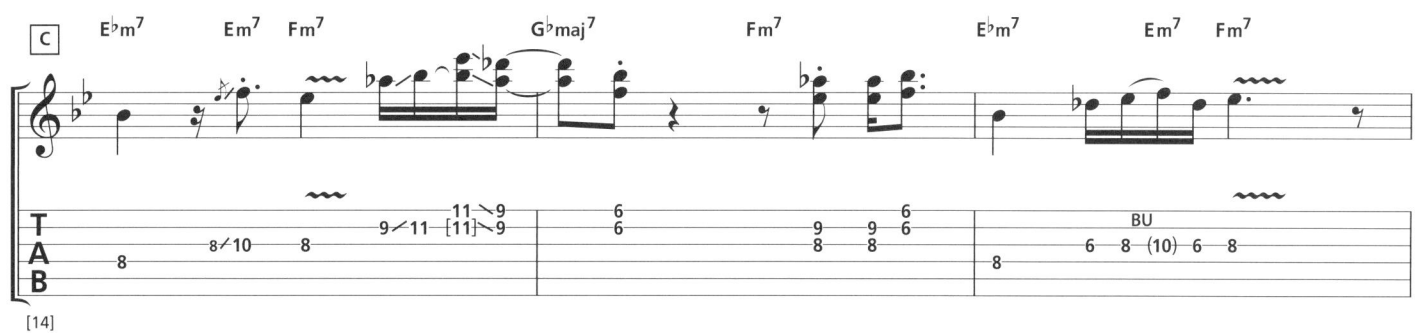
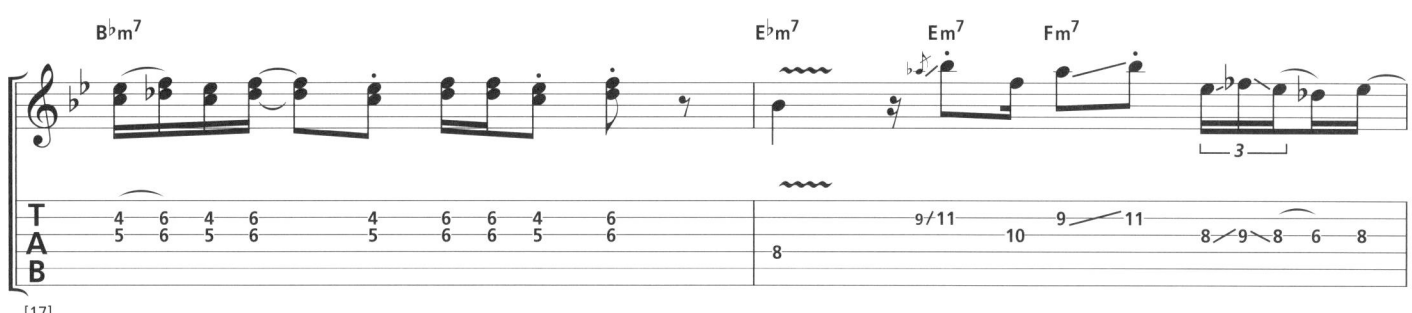
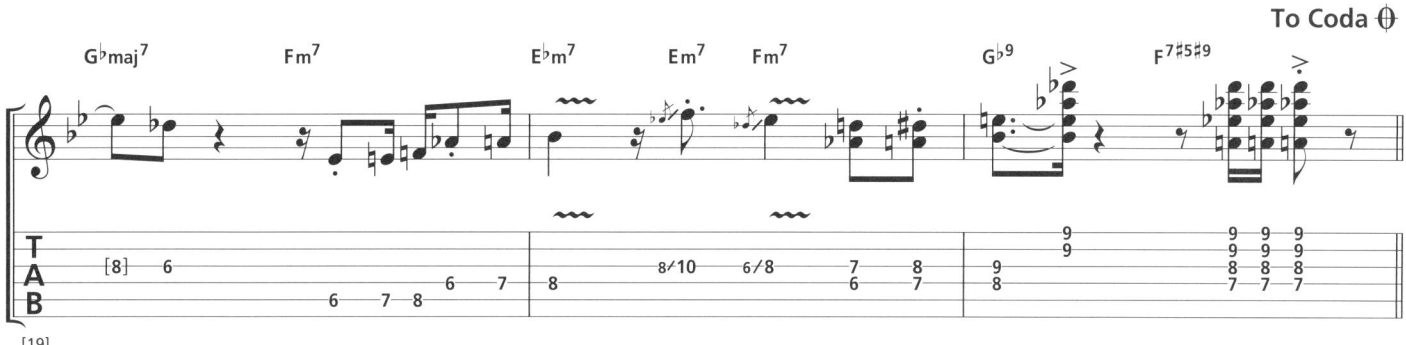
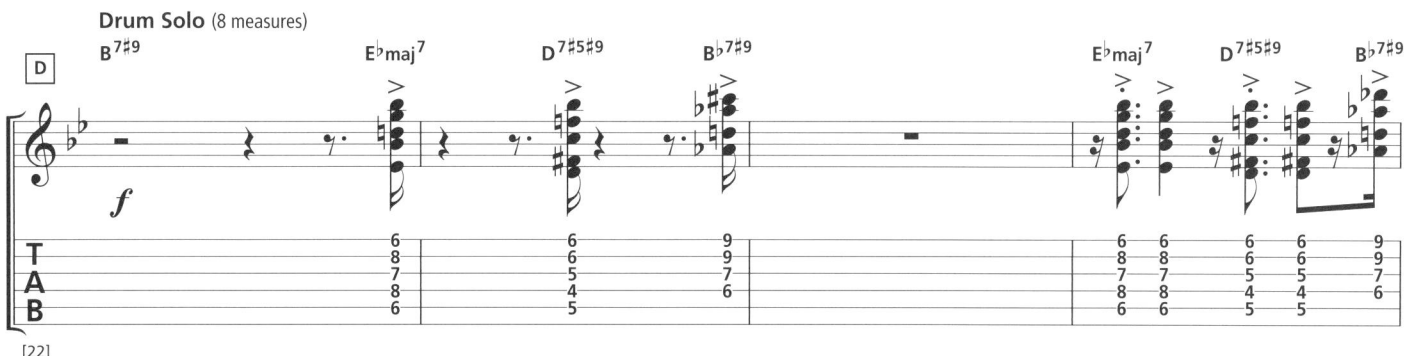
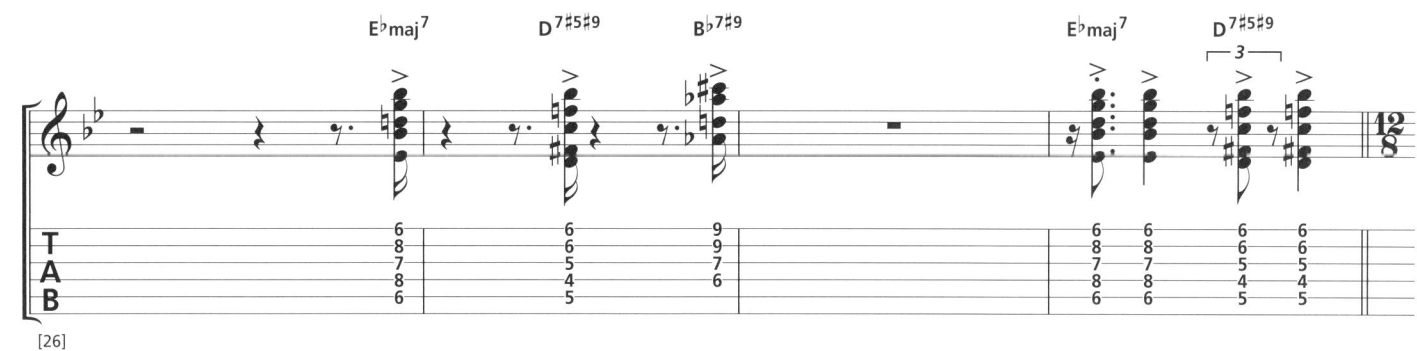

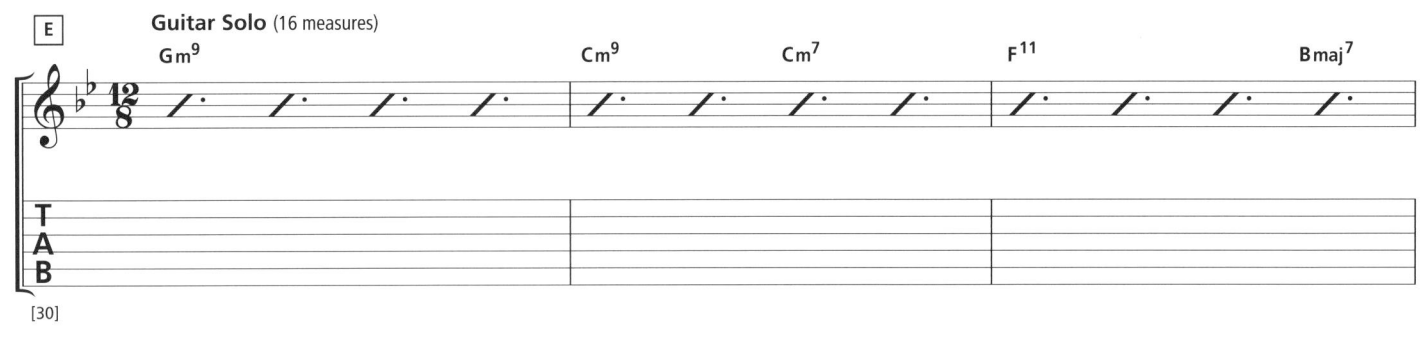
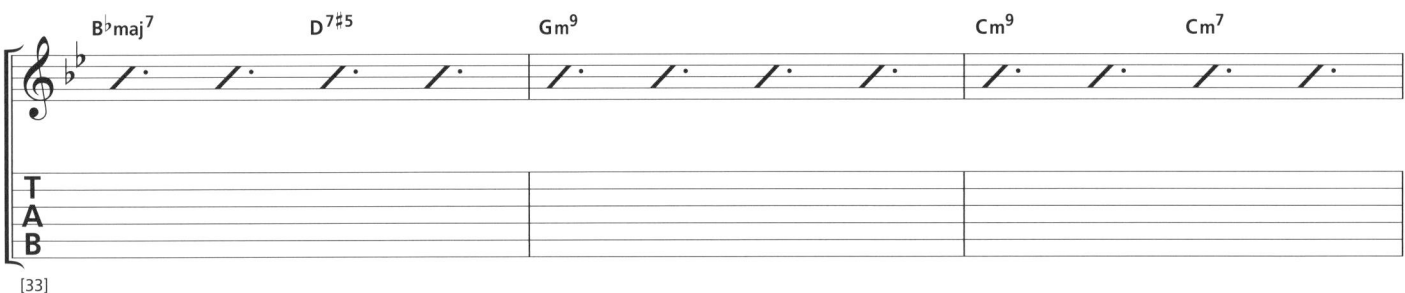
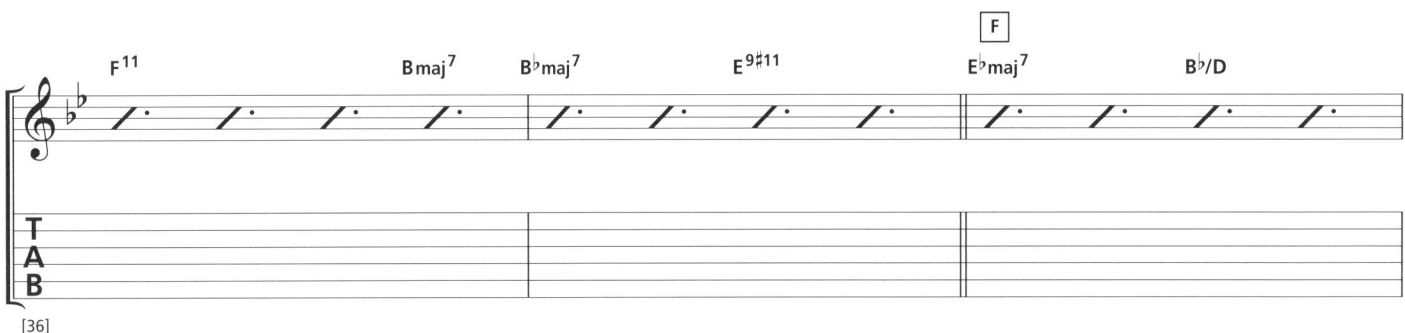
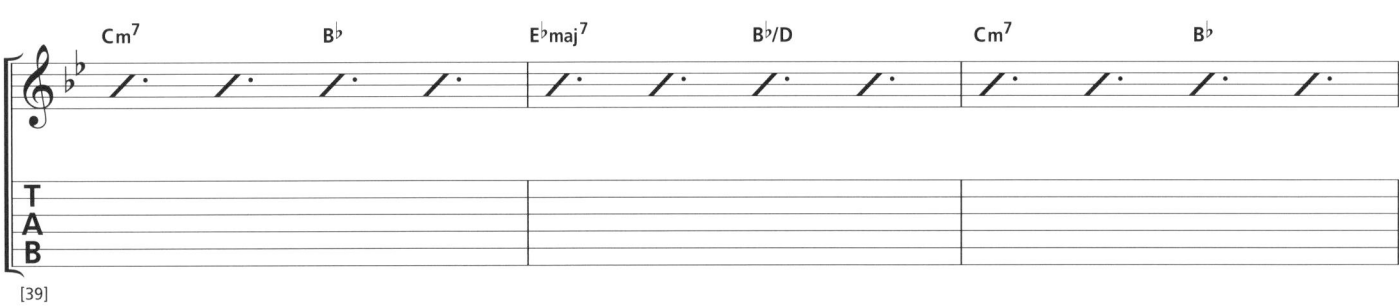
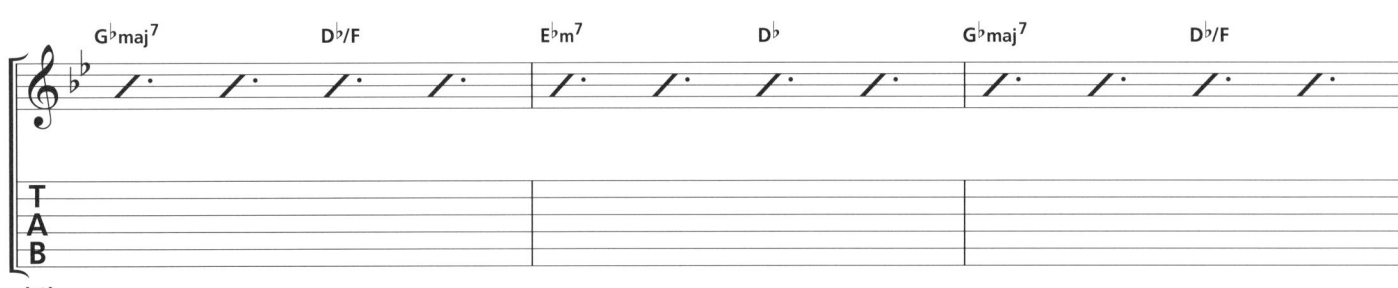

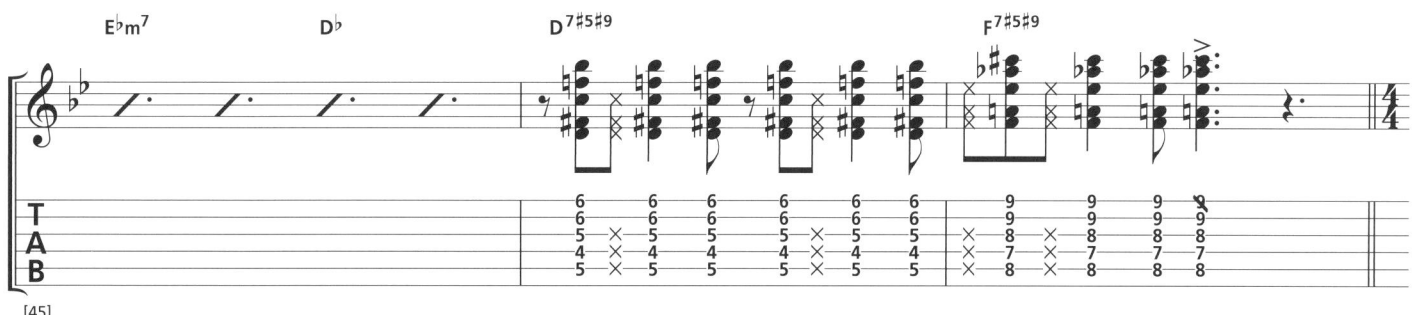
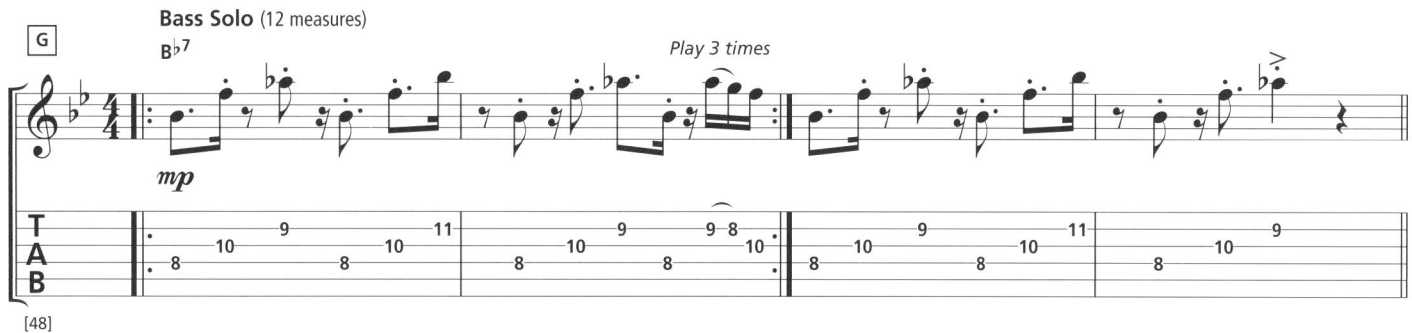
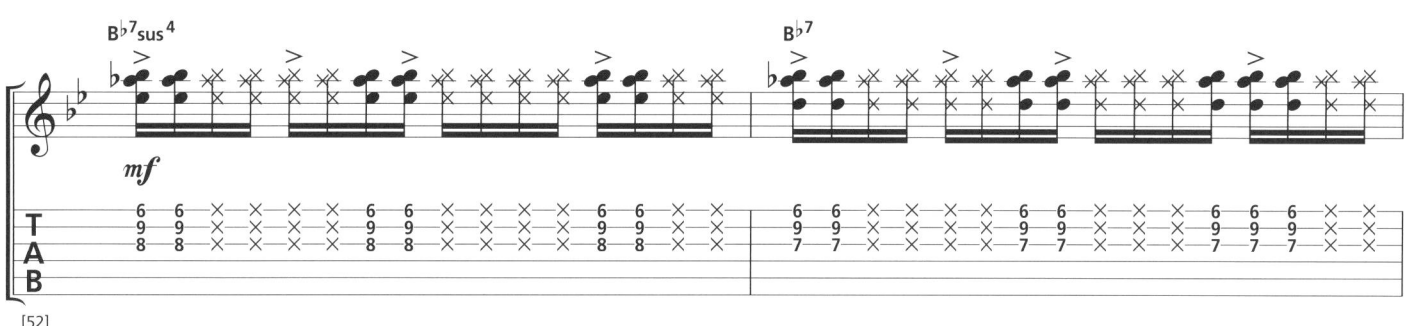
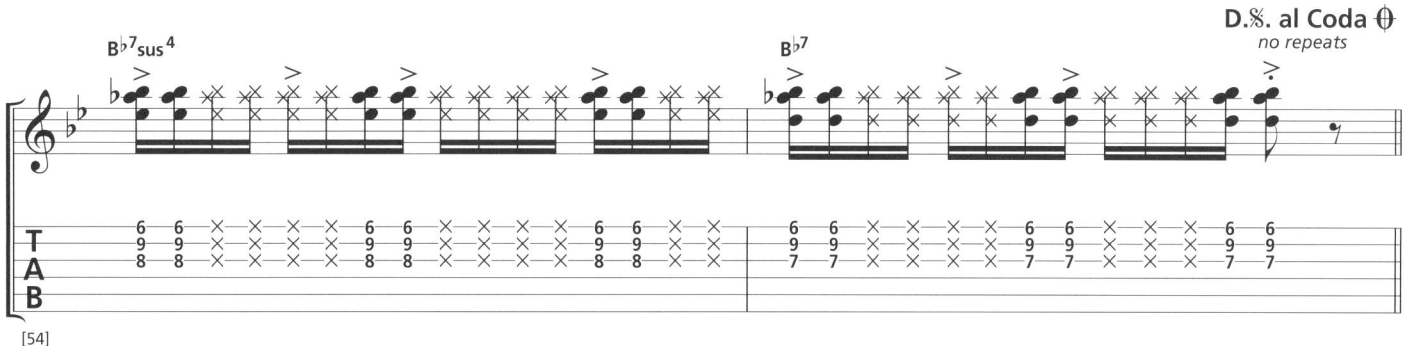
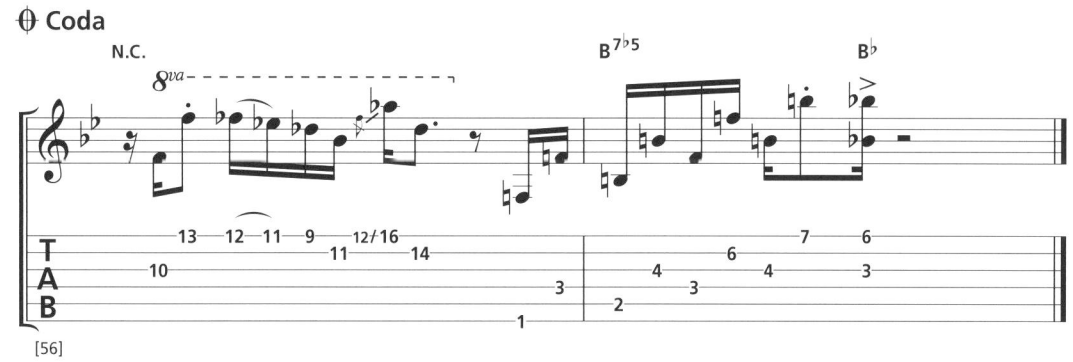

Walkthrough

Amp Settings
A slightly overdriven tone is used on the recording but you can also use a clean tone for the majority of the song and switch to a distorted tone for the guitar solo. Aim for a light overdrive and make sure you retain clarity.

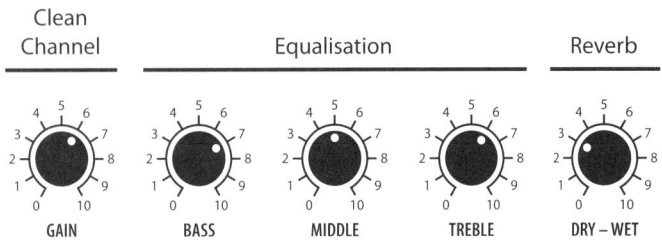

A section (Measures 1–4)
The A section is an accented 16th-note rhythm that uses a combination of three-note chords and muted strings.

Measures 1–4 | *Accents*
The accents in measures 1–4 are trickier to articulate than they may first appear, and the main challenge is to play an accent while your fingers are not holding a chord.

B Section (Measures 5–13)
The B section is a funky, syncopated melody that combines single-note lines with double-stops and chords.

Measures 5–13 | *Playing tightly*
When playing mid-tempo funk tracks guitarists often rush ahead of the beat, especially when there are big gaps between phrases. Relax and aim to really lock in to the groove.

C Section (Measures 14–21)
This syncopated melody uses a range of articulations like staccato notes, double-stop slides and hammer-ons.

Measure 17 | *Double-stop hammer-on*
Fret the E♭ and C notes with your first and second fingers and then hammer-on with the pad of your third finger so that you fret both the B and G strings. Listen closely to ensure both notes ring out because it's easy to miss the B string as you hammer-on (Fig. 1).

D Section (Measures 22–29)
The drum solo is accompanied by heavily syncopated stabs that use extended chords such as the 7♯9 and 7♯5♯9.

Measures 22–29 | *Syncopated stabs*
Avoid rushing accented notes and chords at slow tempos with large rests by using a metronome. Count through the measures, aiming to place each note *exactly* on the correct beat.

E & F Sections (Measures 30–47)
In the E and F sections the song changes to the 12/8 time signature for the guitar solo. The E section is in G minor whereas the F section moves into more modal territory.

Measures 30–45 | *Scale choices*
The first half of the solo is based in G minor and the natural minor will work through the majority of it. The second half is based on the same set of notes but outlines E♭ lydian before the progression modulates to G♭ lydian (they can also be considered as 'standard' major progressions). While the change from G minor to E♭ lydian simply requires a shift of the tonal centre, practise the modulation from E♭ to G♭ otherwise the change in scale may sound unmusical.

G Section (Measures 48–55)
This heavily syncopated single-note line accompanies the bass solo before returning to the groove in the A section.

Measures 48–51 | *Complex rhythms*
You may find this riff easier to learn by ear. Listen closely to the recording for the rhythm. Alternatively, count through the measure in 16th notes (see example in Fig. 2) and work out where in the measure each note falls and practise slowly.

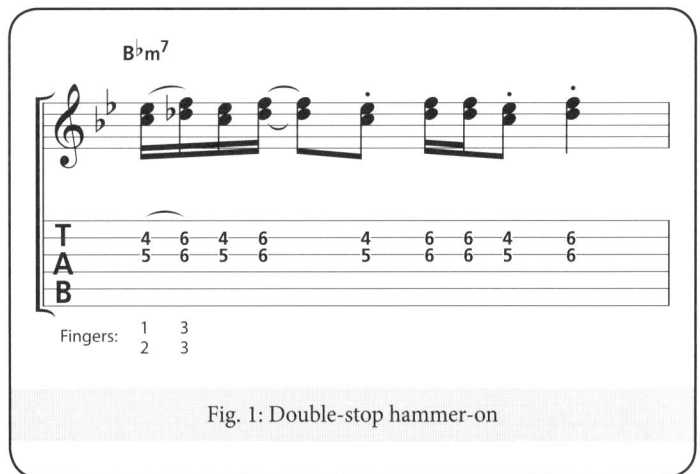

Fig. 1: Double-stop hammer-on

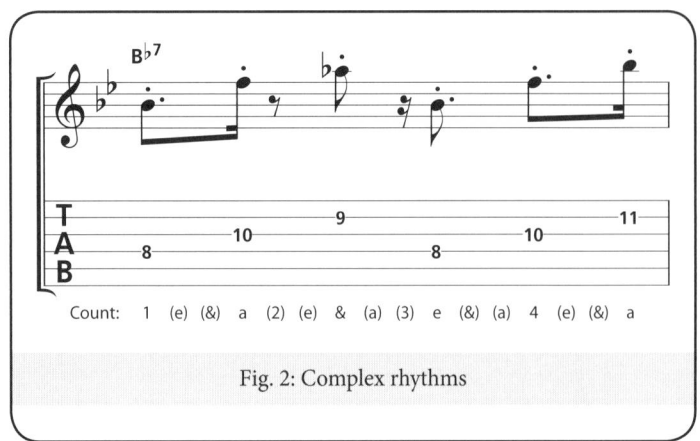

Fig. 2: Complex rhythms

Lead Sheet

SONG TITLE: LEAD SHEET
GENRE: ROCK
TEMPO: 98 BPM
KEY: F# MINOR

TECH FEATURES: OCTAVES
16TH NOTE TRIPLETS
TWO HANDED TAPPING

COMPOSER: JAMES UINGS

PERSONNEL: STUART RYAN (GTR)
DAVE MARKS (BASS)
NOAM LEDERMAN (DRUMS)

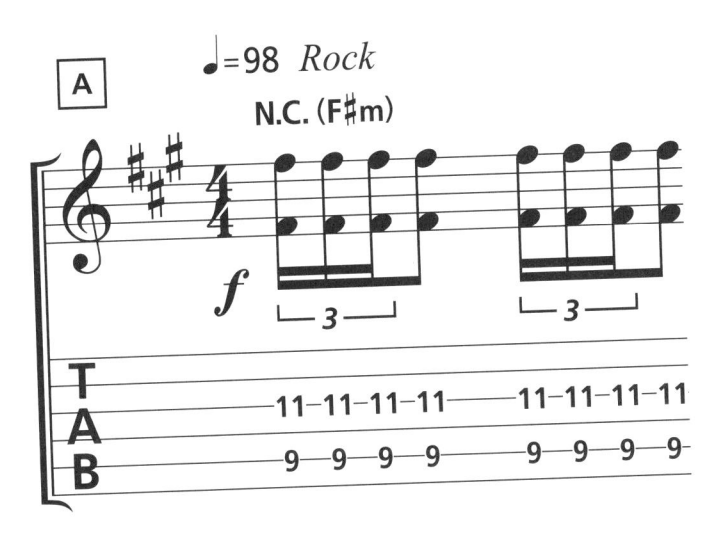

OVERVIEW

'Lead Sheet' is a rap rock track in the style of Rage Against The Machine (RATM), Limp Bizkit and Red Hot Chili Peppers (RHCP). It features octaves, 16th note triplets and two-hand tapping.

STYLE FOCUS

Rap rock bands are influenced by the production of hip hop tracks where producers sample short sections of songs then loop them. As a result, rap rock riffs tend to be small, self-contained cells repeated throughout verse and/or chorus sections. Most of these riffs are based on the minor pentatonic or blues scales. 'Lead Sheet' is set in F# minor and therefore follows a tradition that runs from Led Zeppelin's 'Immigrant Song' to RATM's 'Bombtrack'. Rage guitarist Tom Morello developed a unique style that mimicked a DJ's turntable techniques and was an influence on later bands like Korn and Limp Bizkit.

THE BIGGER PICTURE

Hip hop producers have been sampling rock riffs since the mid 1980s when Run DMC, Public Enemy, and Beastie Boys all scored hits that borrowed from Aerosmith, Slayer and Led Zeppelin. RHCP and RATM saw the potential in this rock rap crossover and combined distorted guitar riffs with rap vocals.

RHCP's album *BloodSugarSexMagik* (1991) spawned the rap rock classics 'Funky Monks', 'Suck My Kiss' and 'Sir Psycho Sexy'. The following year, RATM released their self-titled debut and turned a generation of rockers on to a form of rock where groove and aggression were key.

This next wave of rap rockers included Limp Bizkit and Incubus. Unlike RATM, whose guitarist Tom Morello simulated turntable effects, these groups employed DJs to introduce hip hop techniques including scratching and cutting.

RECOMMENDED LISTENING

RCHP's *BloodSugarSexMagik* is the most rap orientated of their albums. RATM's debut is essential listening, particularly the songs 'Bombtrack', 'Bullet In The Head' and 'Know Your Enemy'. 'Bulls On Parade', from their 1996 follow-up *Evil Empire*, is also recommended. Limp Bizkit's *Chocolate Starfish And The Hotdog Flavoured Water* (2000) is worth investigating for 'My Generation', 'Rollin'' and 'Take A Look Around'.

Lead Sheet

James Uings

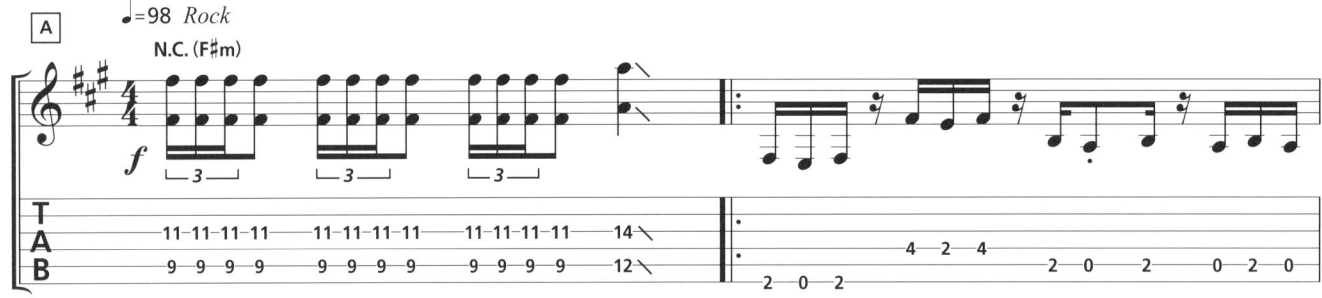
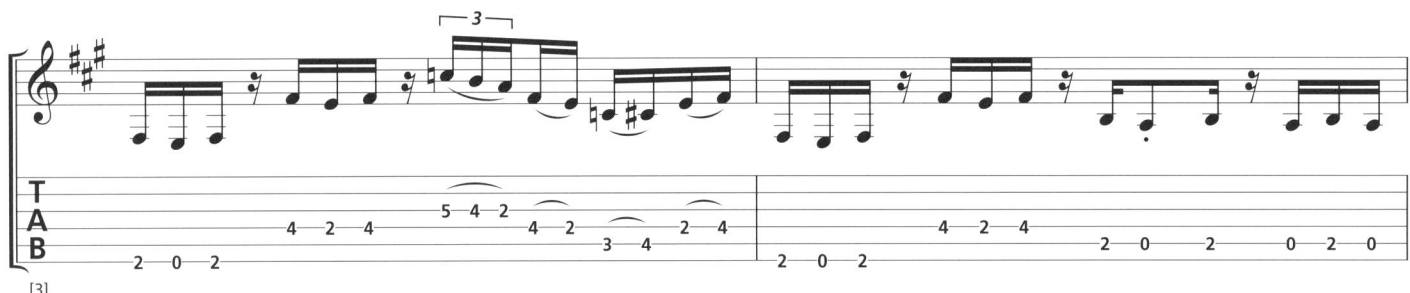
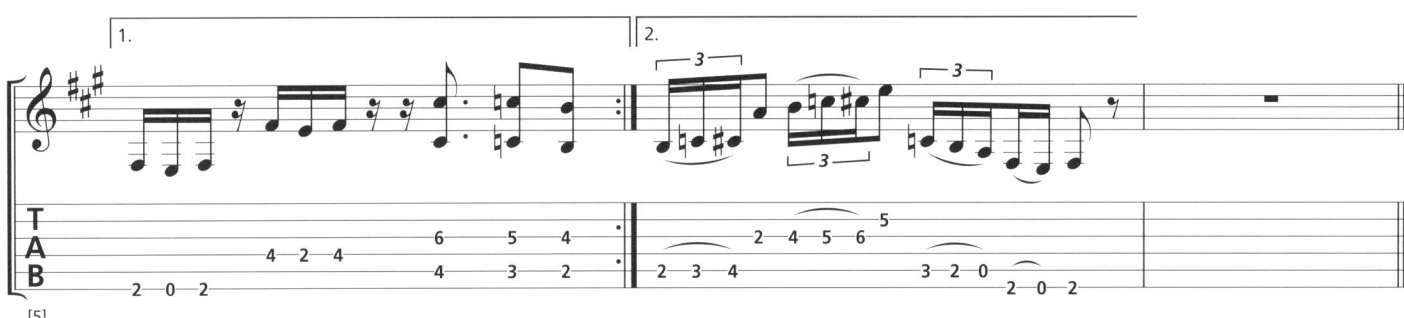
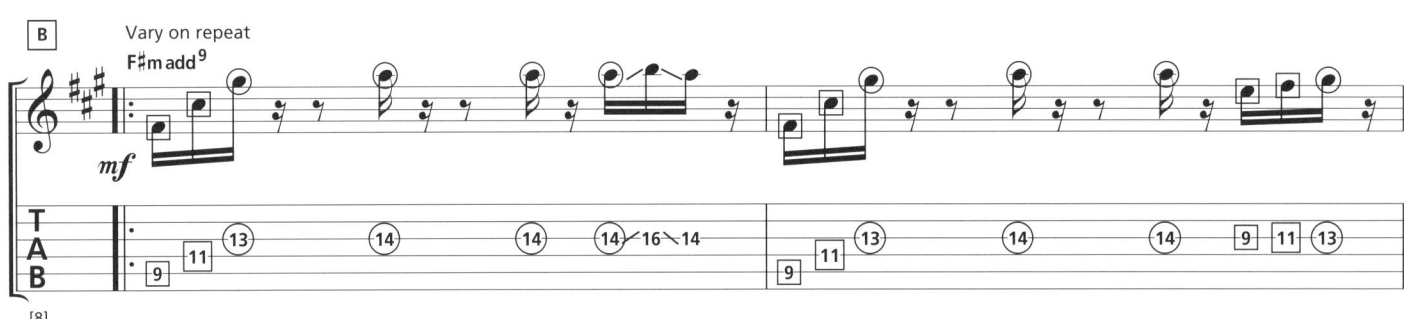
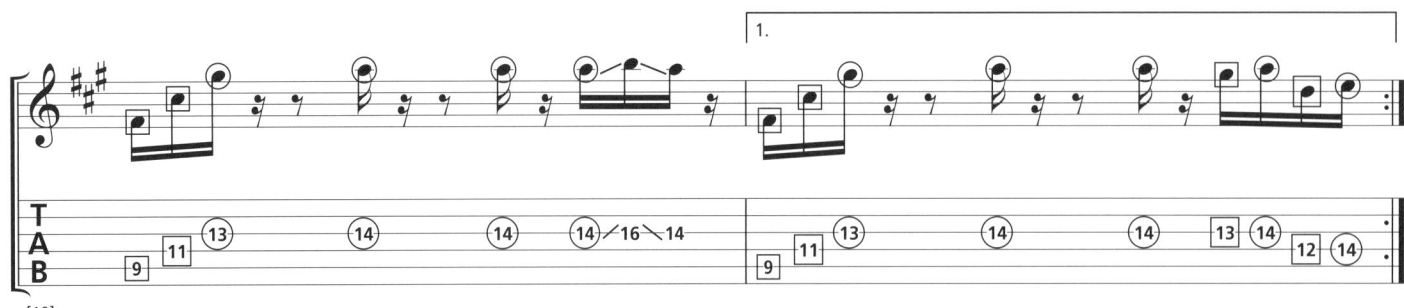

© Copyright 2012 Rock School Ltd.

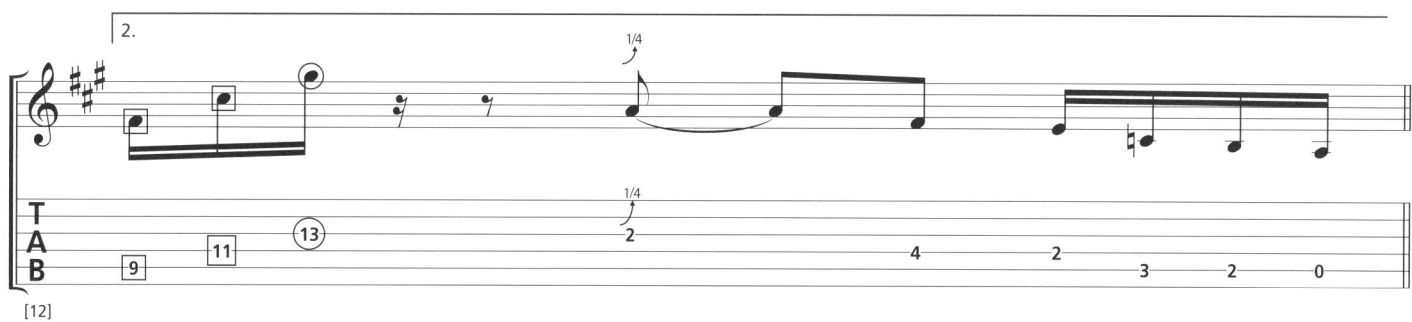

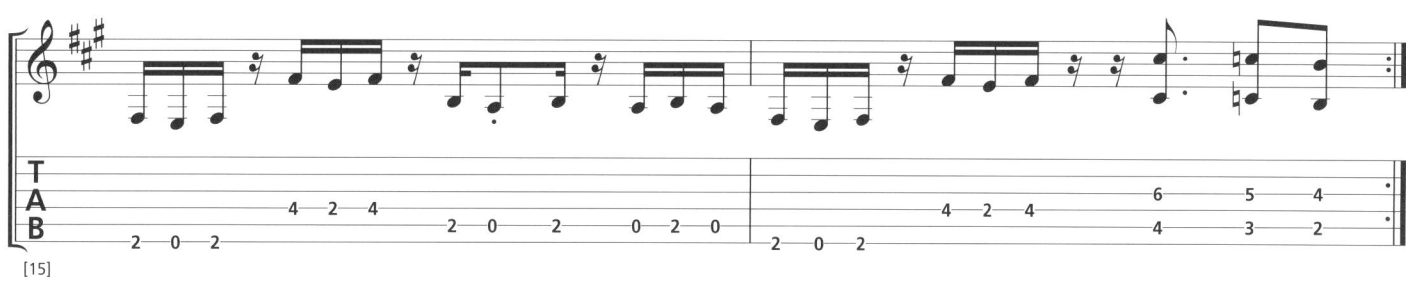
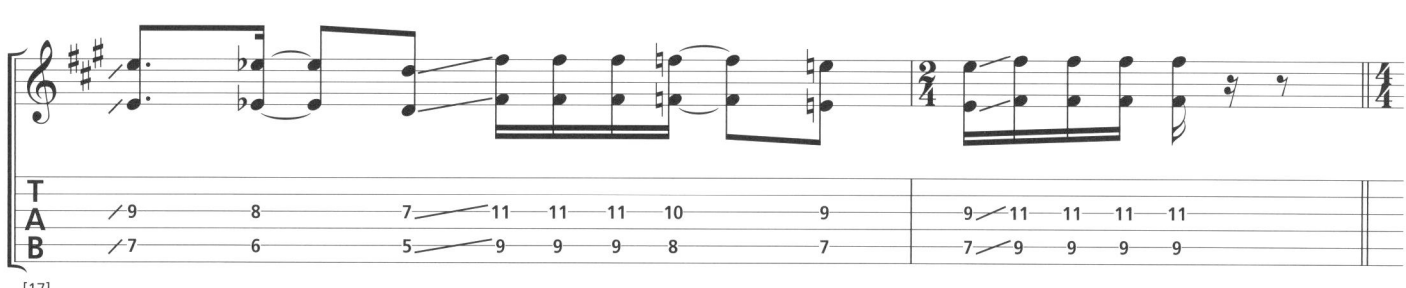

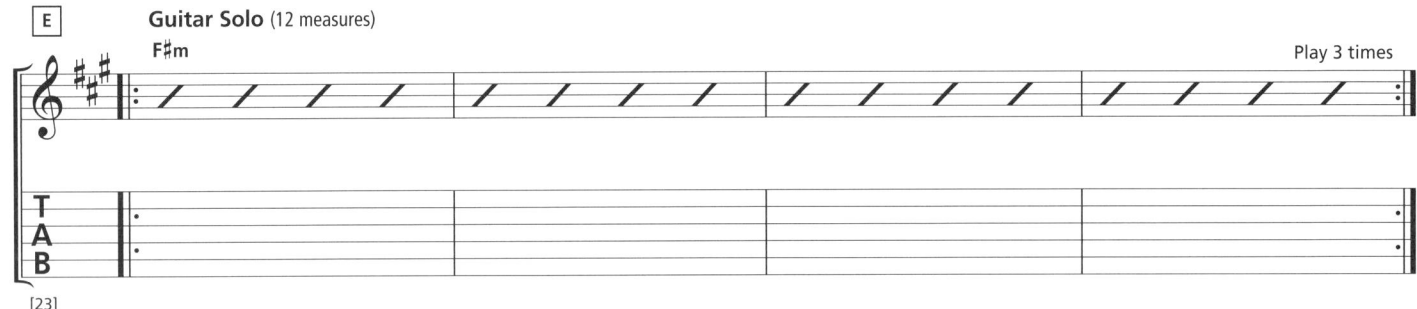
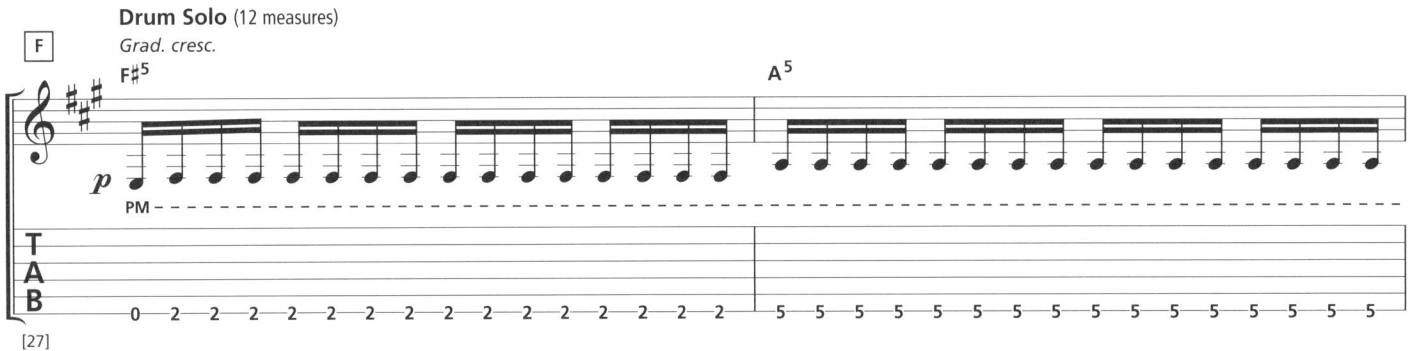
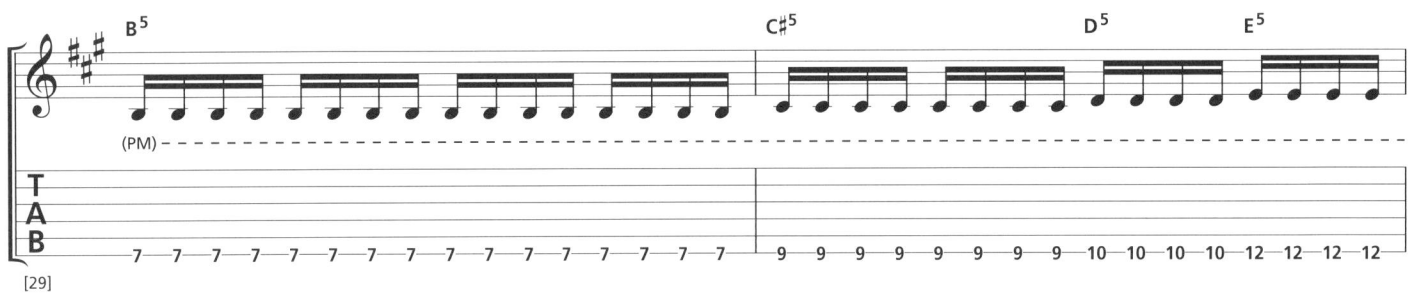
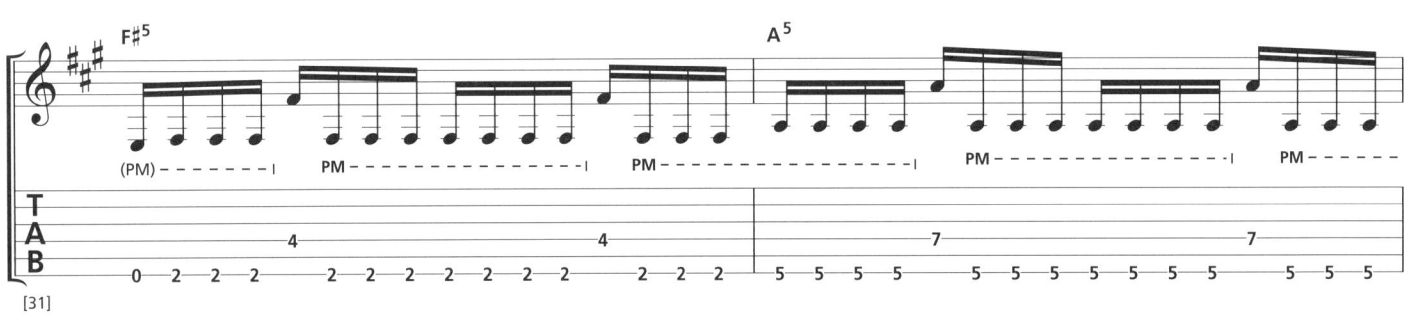
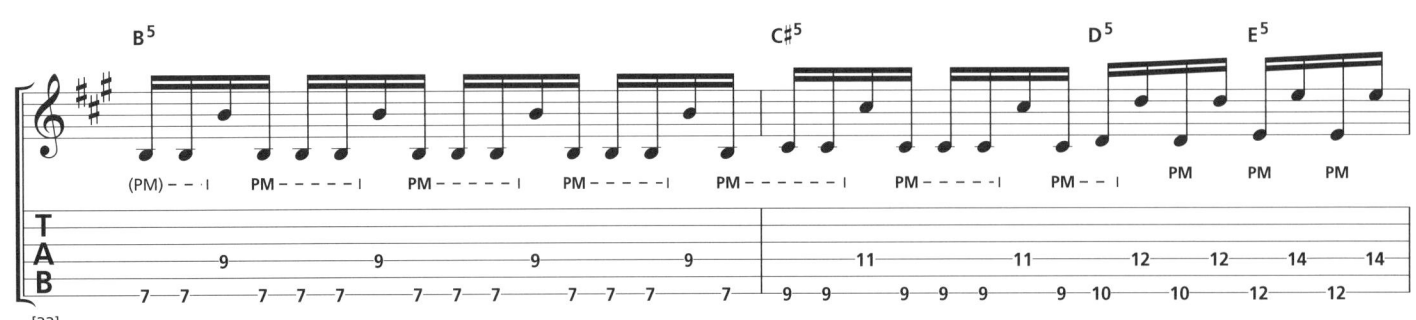

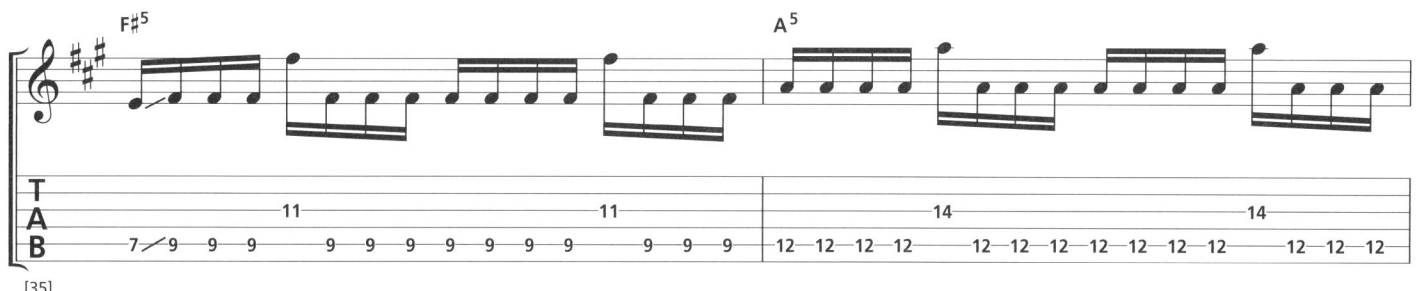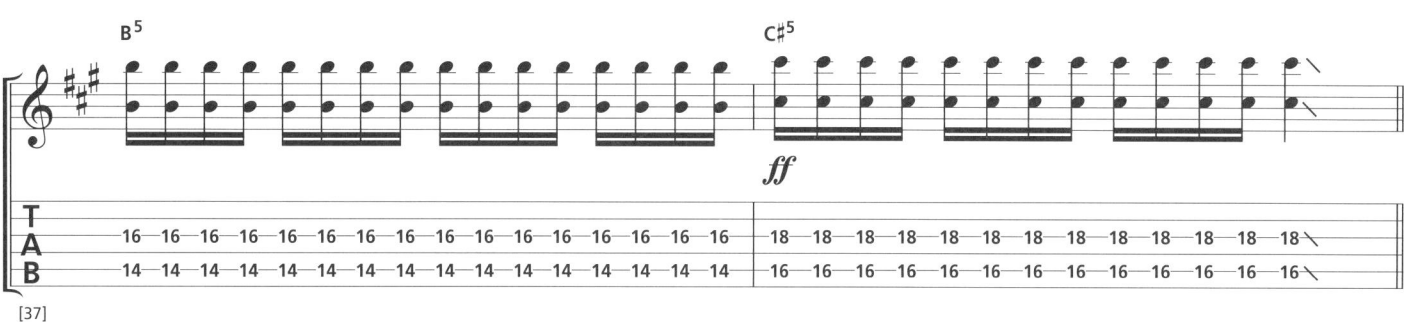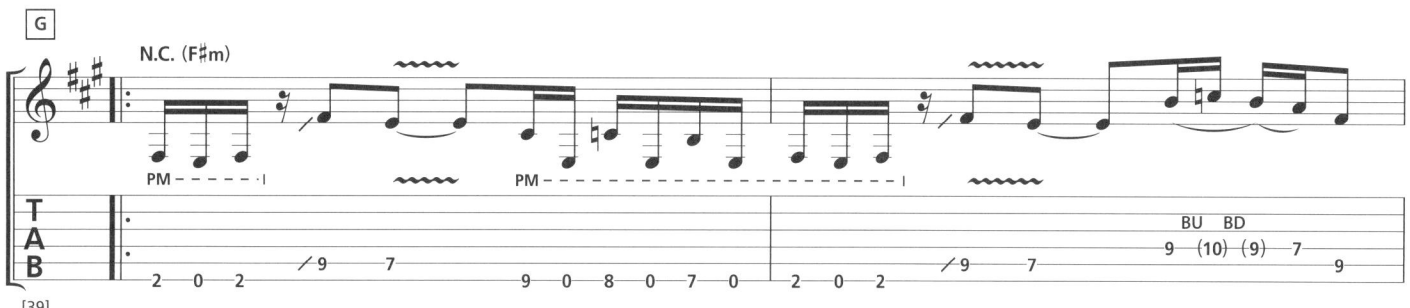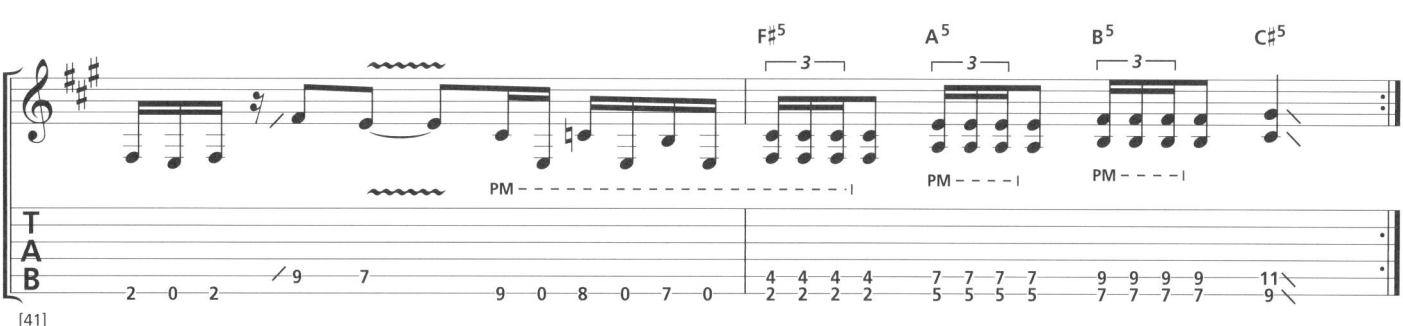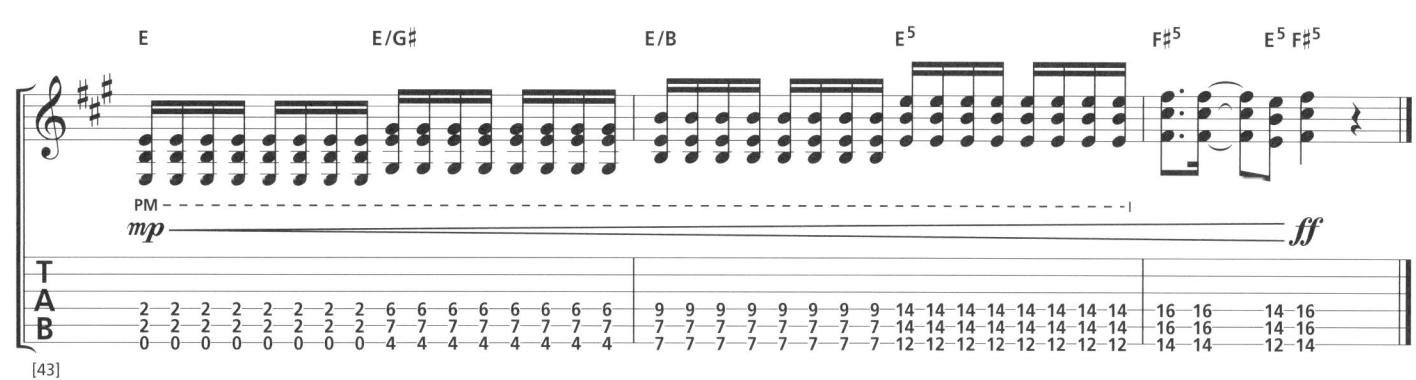

Walkthrough

Amp Settings

Use a modern high-gain distortion but set the gain a little lower than you would on most other kinds of rock and metal. You may wish to add some delay in the tapped sections and boost the gain for the guitar solo.

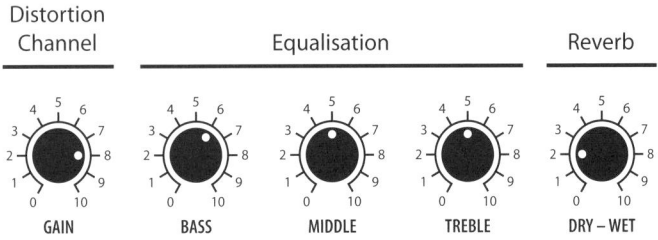

A Section (Measures 1–7)

The A section starts with octaves played in unison with the bass and drums before moving to a syncopated single-note riff based on the blues scale.

Measure 1 | *16th-note triplets*
The fast octaves to be found in this measure are best played with a down up down up strumming action for each set of four notes. This means that the final eighth note will then be played using an upstroke, which may feel uncomfortable at first (Fig. 1).

Measure 3 | *Legato phrasing*
The first three notes of beat 3 are undoubtedly the most challenging of this phrase. The two pull-offs should be executed as one smooth movement by snapping your fretting hand towards the floor. Even though it is one overall motion, make sure both pull-offs sound cleanly as it is common for the second note to be lost in this kind of lick.

B & C Sections (Measures 8–18)

The A section uses two-handed tapping to outline the chords and play a melody line. The C section is a reprise of the A section.

Measures 8–13 | *Two-handed tapping*
The first two notes of each measure are played by hammering your fretting fingers onto the fretboard without picking (marked with a square). Hammer down firmly to make a clean contact and avoid unwanted string noise. Notes that are circled are tapped with the picking hand. This riff will take a while to co-ordinate so start slowly and gradually build up speed.

D & E Sections (Measures 19–26)

The D section is the bass solo where the guitar plays stabs with the drums. The E section is the guitar solo.

Measures 23–26 | *Guitar solo*
This 12-measure solo is played over a repeated blues scale riff played by the bass. With a solo of this length over a riff that implies a single chord, it is easy to fall into playing collections of licks rather than creating a coherent musical idea. You will need to plan out a basic structure (even if you improvise within this) to build an effective solo that has direction and complements the song.

F & G Sections (Measures 27–45)

The F section is the drum solo, over which the guitar plays a part that builds in volume and intensity. The G section is a riff that uses heavy palm muting, 16th note triplets, and climaxes with a gradual build using three-note chords moving through different inversions of the E chord.

Measure 34 | *Fast octave picking*
This measure features some fast string skipping. Strict alternate picking is undoubtedly the way to play this phrase (Fig. 2). You should also work to minimise the motion in your picking action to play this challenging phrase up to speed.

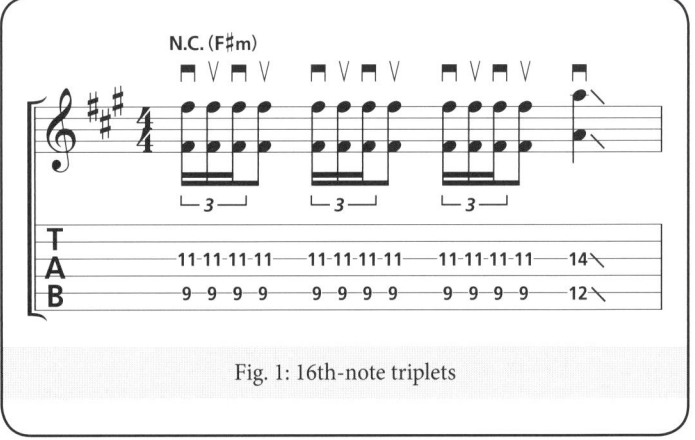

Fig. 1: 16th-note triplets

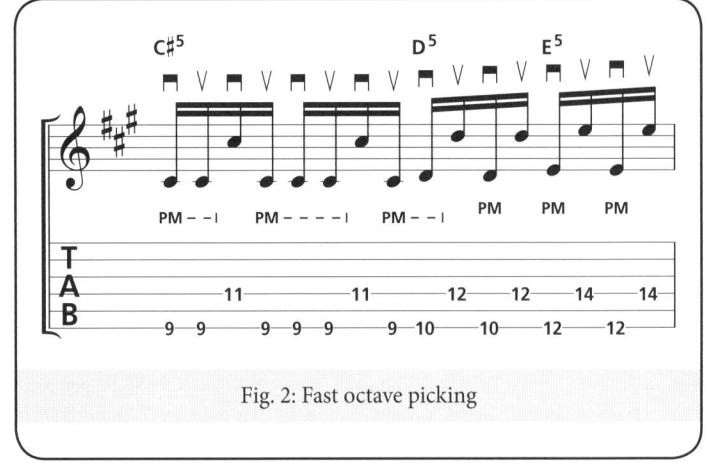

Fig. 2: Fast octave picking

Freightshaker

SONG TITLE: FREIGHTSHAKER
GENRE: BLUES
TEMPO: 160 BPM
KEY: A MINOR (BLUES)

TECH FEATURES: FAST TRIPLET LICKS
9TH CHORDS
ARPEGGIATED CHORDS

COMPOSER: SIMON TROUP

PERSONNEL: STUART RYAN (GTR)
HENRY THOMAS (BASS)
NOAM LEDERMAN (DRUMS)
ROSS STANLEY (KEYS)

OVERVIEW

'Freightshaker' is an uptempo blues composition with a strong Texan influence à la Stevie Ray Vaughan, Kenny Wayne Sheppard and Walter Trout. It features fast triplet licks, sophisticated accompaniment chords, and heavily swung riffing among its techniques.

STYLE FOCUS

Fast Texan blues is exciting and poses some technical challenges for you to enjoy. In the trio format, timing, touch and tone have to be spot on: if you lose your place it can be difficult to get back onboard. Dynamics are also critical when playing within the trio format. Here, for example, knowing when to dig in and when to sit back is the difference between a good and a great performance. As a rule, sitting back while the other instruments solo and digging in harder for your own solo works well. This style of blues requires a heavier guitar tone and a strong pick attack, as demonstrated by Vaughan.

THE BIGGER PICTURE

Although he was by no means the first, Vaughan is considered the greatest of the Texan bluesmen. He rose to fame after he and his band Double Trouble were discovered by Jackson Browne and David Bowie at the Montreaux Jazz Festival of 1982. Influenced a great deal by Jimi Hendrix, Vaughan's knowledge of the blues was encyclopedic and his technique was more adept than even his hero's.

After supplying the Albert King style licks for Bowie's *Let's Dance*, Vaughan was offered the lead guitar slot in a two year tour with Bowie but turned it down to prioritise his own band. Their 1983 debut, *Texas Flood*, should be a cornerstone of any self-respecting blues fan's record collection.

Vaughan died in a helicopter accident in August 1990, but his playing still inspires young blues players like Kenny Wayne Sheppard and Philip Sayce.

RECOMMENDED LISTENING

To hear the uptempo side of blues, take a listen to Vaughan's 'Testify' or 'Scuttle Buttin'. Joe Bonamassa also plays with great technique and control at higher speeds as displayed on tracks like 'Travellin' South' from his 2004 album *Had To Cry Today*. Blues rock legend Gary Moore was especially adept at high speed blues riffing and soloing, as heard on *Blues Alive* (1993) and the guitar solo on 'Walking By Myself.'

Freightshaker

Simon Troup

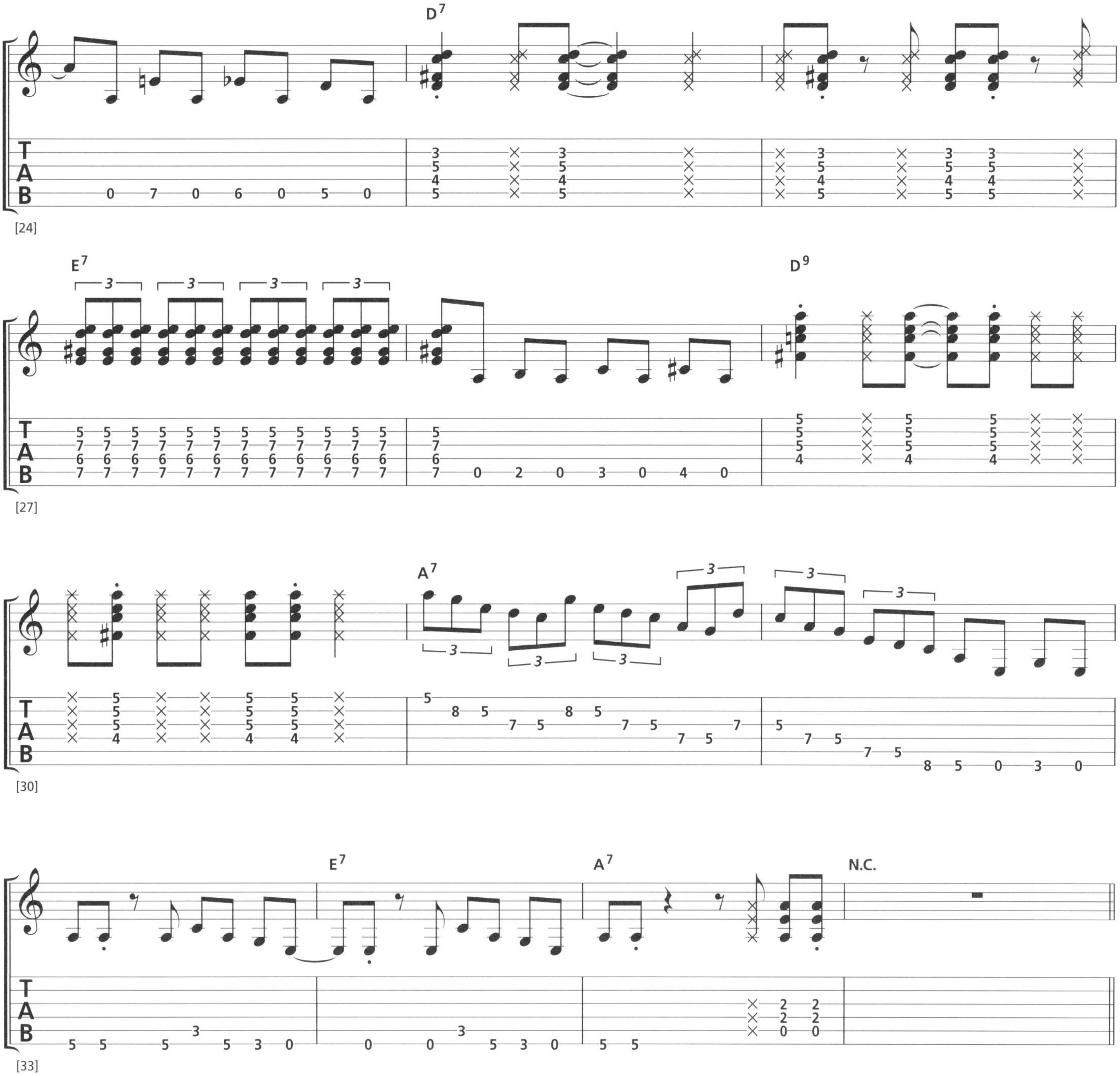

D **Guitar Solo** (16 measures)

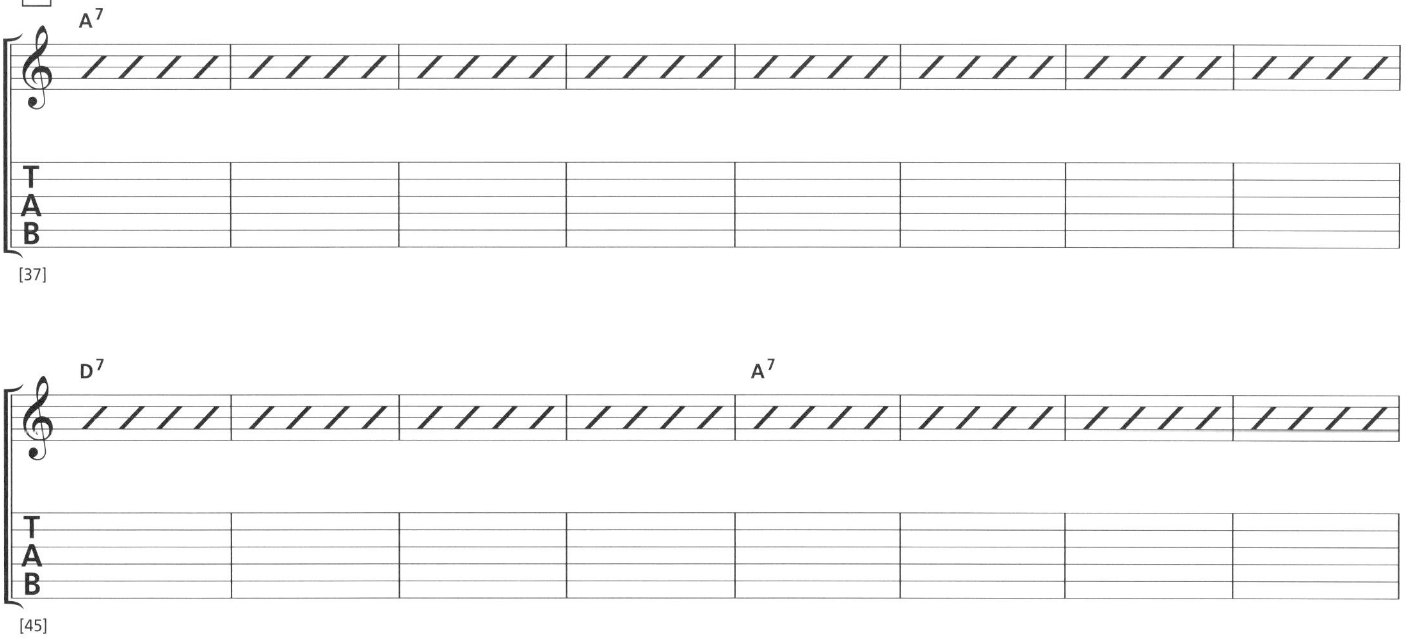

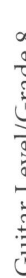

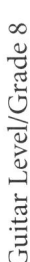

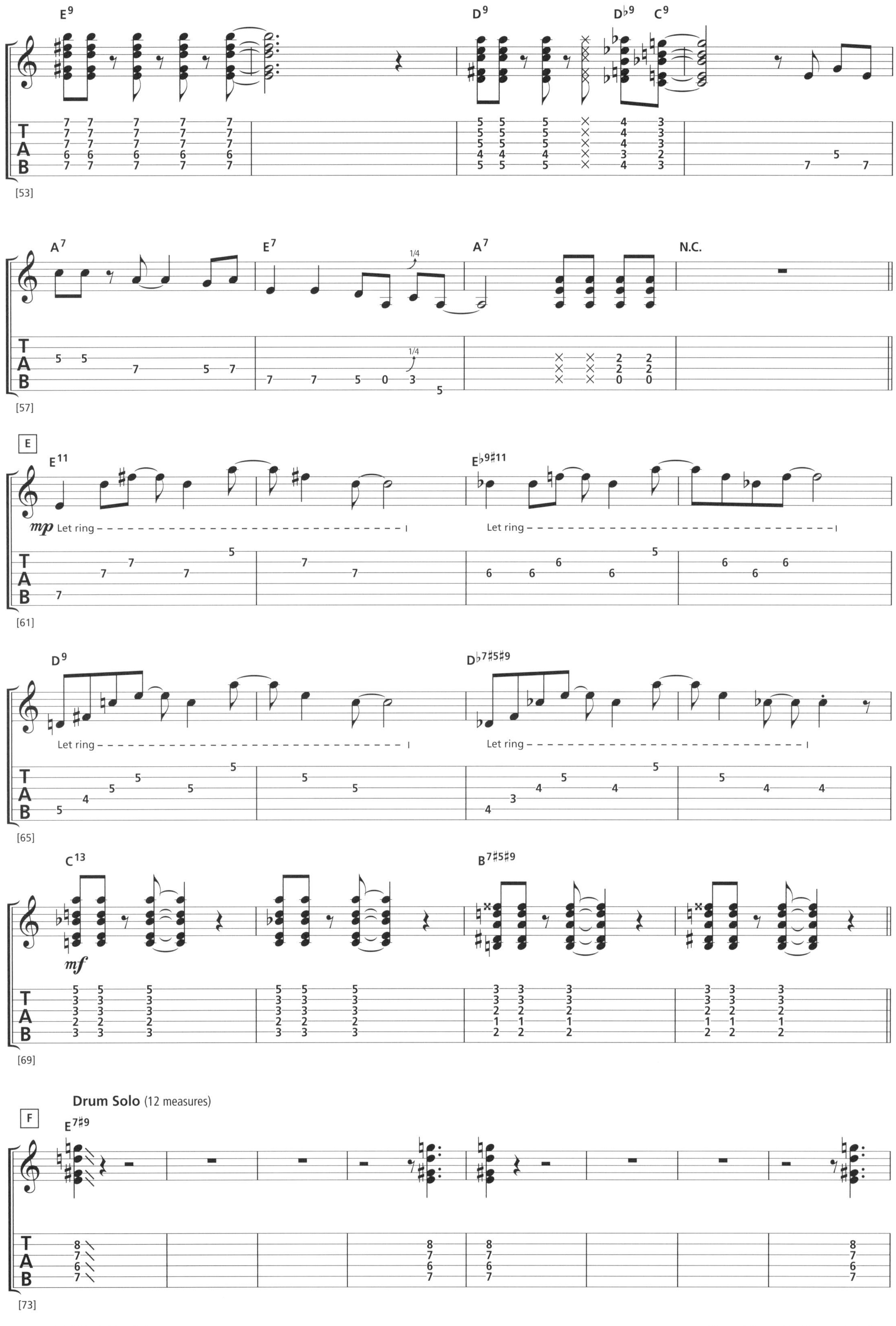
E9
D9
D♭9
C9
[53]
A7
E7
1/4
A7
N.C.
[57]
E
E11
mp
Let ring
E♭9♯11
Let ring
[61]
D9
Let ring
D♭7♯5♯9
Let ring
[65]
C13
mf
B7♯5♯9
[69]
Drum Solo (12 measures)
F
E7♯9
[73]

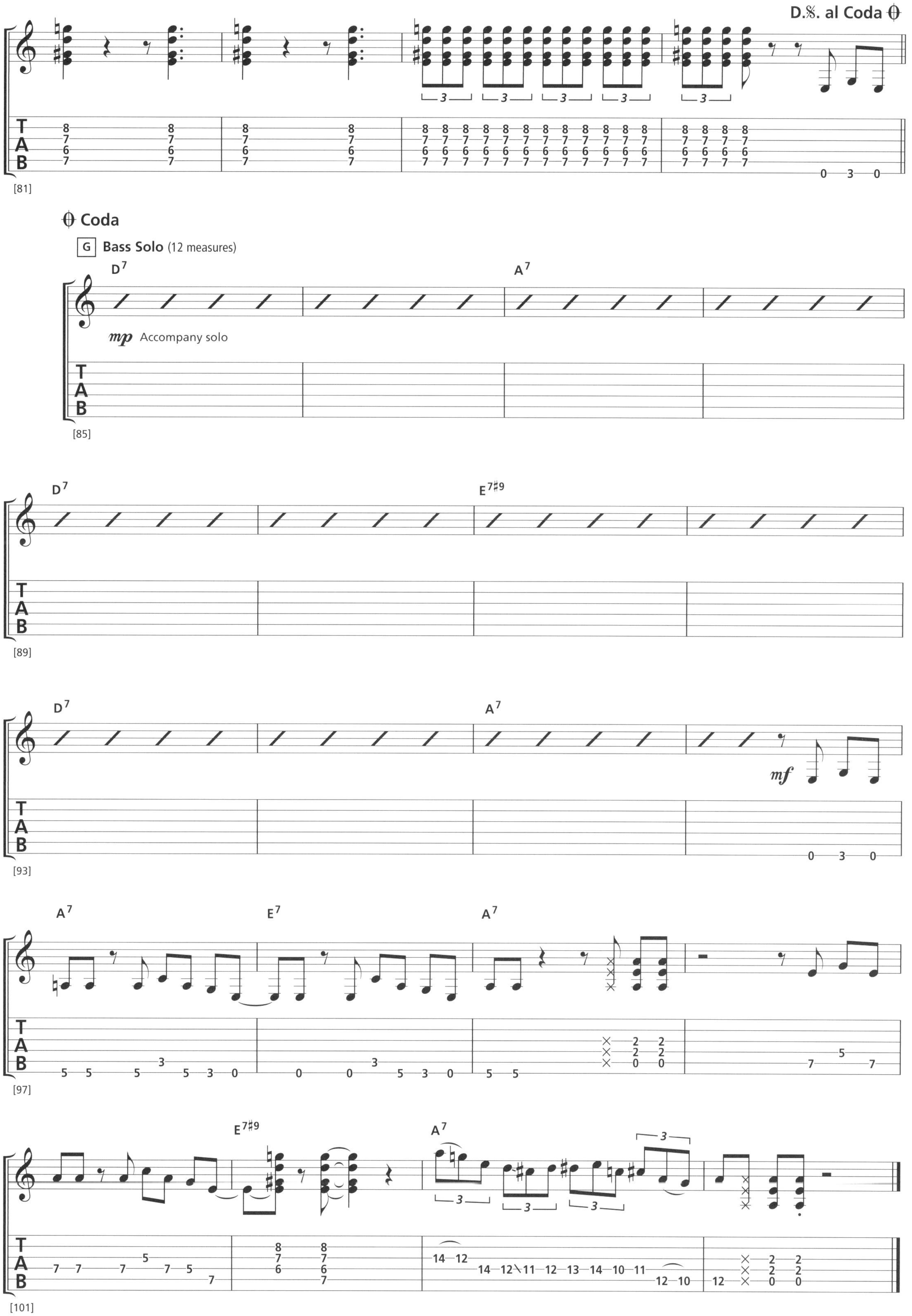
D.𝄋. al Coda
[81]
Coda
G Bass Solo (12 measures)
D7
A7
mp Accompany solo
[85]
D7
E7♯9
[89]
D7
A7
mf
[93]
A7
E7
A7
[97]
E7♯9
A7
[101]

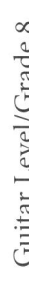

Walkthrough

Amp Settings

Opt for an aggressive, overdriven tone with plenty of bite. Set the gain quite high and boost the middle to help the guitar's sound cut through the mix, particularly during the solo. You can either switch to a clean tone for the quieter sections or simply turn your guitar's volume control down to produce a less distorted tone.

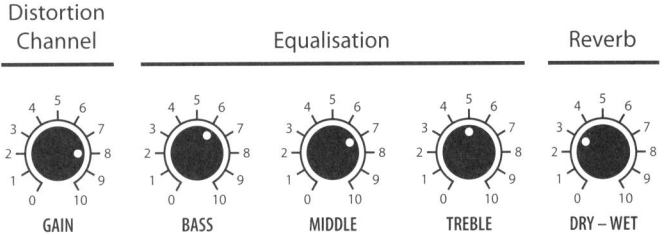

A Section (Measures 1–4)

The A section consists of double-stops played in a syncopated rhythm with heavy vibrato.

Measures 1–4 | *Double-stop vibrato*

Barre the B and G strings with the pad of your first finger and apply vibrato as you play the notated rhythm. Make sure movement is even and consistent and that both strings ring out throughout the phrase.

B & C sections (Measures 5–36)

The B and C sections are bluesy riffs that use single notes, double-stops and staccato 9th chords.

Measure 8 | *Trill*

Trills are indicated by the sign above the notation (Fig. 1). When you see this you should rapidly alternate between the two notes shown in brackets. In this case, the trill is articulated with hammer-ons and pull-offs on the G string while the D string rings alongside the trill.

Measures 23 | *Double-stop legato lick*

Barre your first finger across the E, B and G strings at the fifth fret and play the D on the G string with your third finger. Play the G string with your pick and use one of your picking hand fingers to pluck the E string. Perform the fast legato run with your third and fourth fingers. The final note is played using the still-barred first finger, and the E string should ring out until beat 2.

Measures 31–32 | *Fast triplet run*

Play this high speed phrase using alternate picking (Fig. 2). Use a relaxed picking action and minimise excess motion – your pick should only travel a small amount past the string. Work on these phrases with the metronome set to a lower speed and only increase it when you can play accurately.

D Section (Measures 37–60)

The D section is a 16-measure guitar solo in the key of A. Your main challenge will be creating a solo that is convincing stylistically and suitable for the level/grade.

Measures 37–60 | *Guitar solo*

Blues is generally predisposed to blues scale and minor pentatonic licks, so the A minor pentatonic and blues scales will work here. However, at this level/grade you may wish to explore more advanced ideas. One option is to use the relevant mixolydian mode over each dominant 7 chord. However, another option is to base your ideas on dominant 7 or dominant 9 arpeggios.

E, F & G Sections (61–104)

The E section starts with arpeggiated extended chords before moving to choppy rhythms. The F section features the drum solo and the B section is repeated, giving you the opportunity to vary the part. The G section contains the bass solo where you can create your own accompaniment.

Measures 85–96 | *Accompanying a solo*

This is where you compose an accompaniment for the bass solo. While you must craft an interesting part, remember that your primary goal is to support the soloist.

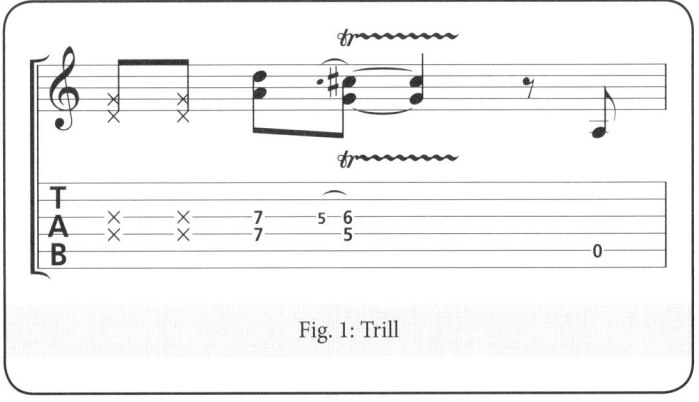

Fig. 1: Trill

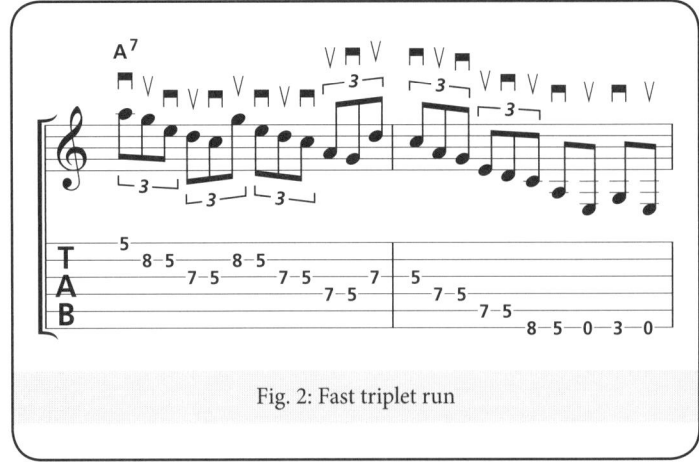

Fig. 2: Fast triplet run

Nosso Samba

SONG TITLE: NOSSO SAMBA
GENRE: SAMBA
TEMPO: 110 BPM
KEY: G MAJOR

TECH FEATURES: FINGERPICKED CHORDS
16TH NOTE STRUMMING

COMPOSER: NOAM LEDERMAN

PERSONNEL: NOAM LEDERMAN (DRUMS)
HENRY THOMAS (BASS)
STUART RYAN (GTR)
KISHON KHAN (KEYS)
FERGUS GERRAND (PERC)
CHRIS WEBSTER (TROMBONE)

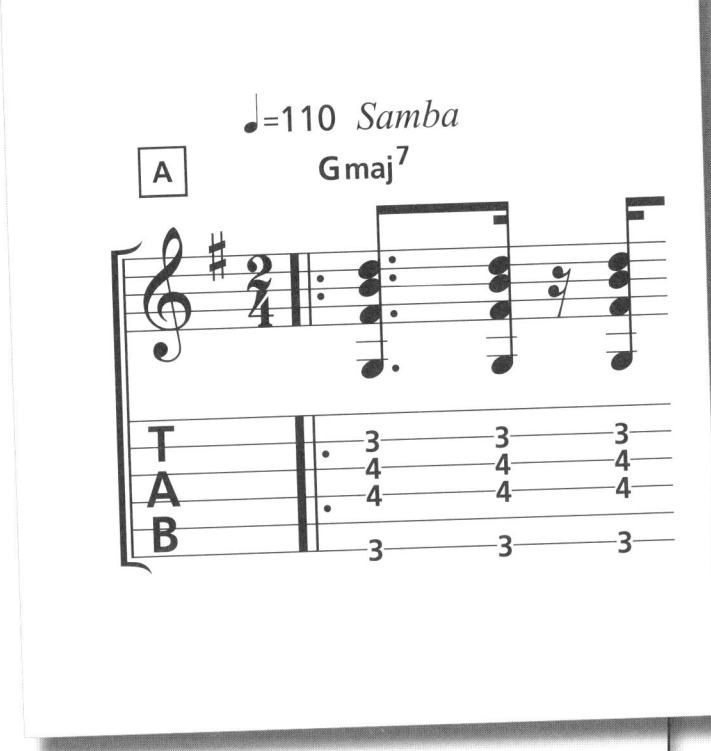

OVERVIEW

'Nosso Samba' is written in the style of classic Brazilian artists such as the revered Antonio Carlos Jobim and Gilberto Gil, and the modern day samba group Nosso Trio. It features octave melodies, fingerpicked chords and 16th note strumming patterns among its techniques.

STYLE FOCUS

Since the bossa nova era of the 1950s, samba has had much in common with jazz. A lot of the music is improvised so a familiarity with playing over standards and changes will be of benefit to a student of the Brazilian music 'Nosso Samba' is based on. The bossa nova rhythm style is usually played with thumb and fingers, although you could achieve the same effect using a combination of pick and fingers.

THE BIGGER PICTURE

Samba is the rhythmic, syncopated music of Brazil with its roots in the African culture of the country's black population. The first samba record is believed to be a song called 'Pelo Telefono' that was released in 1917, and gave the style its first significant exposure outside of the favelas (slums). Early samba relied on the power of drums and percussion, and was revered for its raw energy rather than musical sophistication.

However, this changed in the 1950s when young middle class suburbanites like João Gilberto and Jobim brought in supple melodies and jazz influenced harmonies. This new style, or 'bossa nova', exposed Brazilian music to the world; its best known song is 'The Girl From Ipanema', which was translated into English and performed by Frank Sinatra.

More recently, Nosso Trio have developed modern samba and inspired instrumentalists from every corner of the planet to explore Brazilian music. The trio's guitarist, Nelson Faria, attended Los Angeles' Guitar Institute Of Technology where he studied under fusion guitarists Scott Henderson and Frank Gambale. He has since written books and produced videos about Brazilian guitar playing.

RECOMMENDED LISTENING

Gilberto's *Chega De Saudade* (1959) is a bossa nova classic. To hear how Brazilian music changed in the 1960s, listen to *Caetano Veloso* (1968) by Caetano Veloso. Finally, Nosso Trio's modern take on samba can be heard on their 2006 debut *Vento Bravo*.

Nosso Samba

Noam Lederman

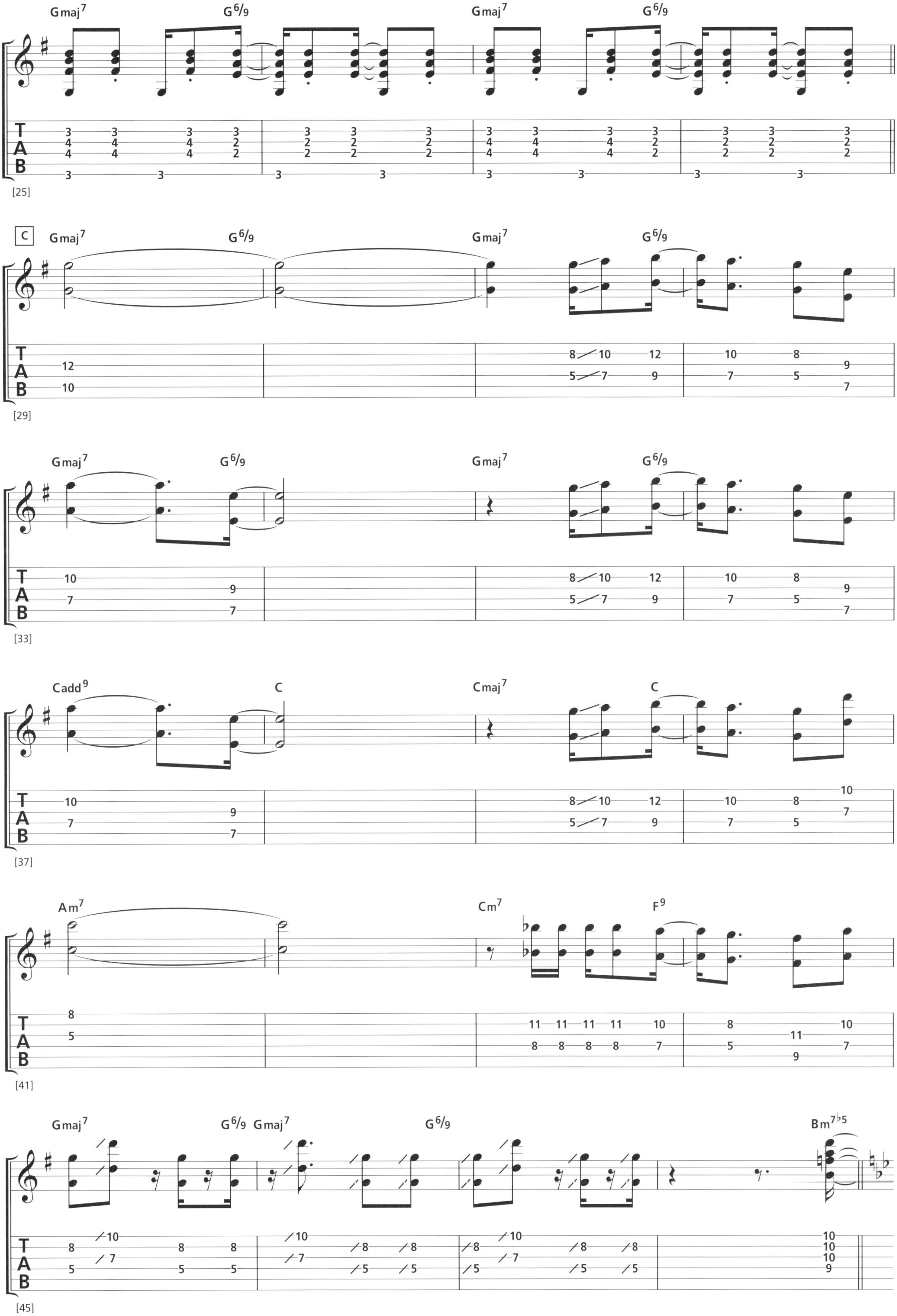

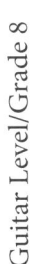

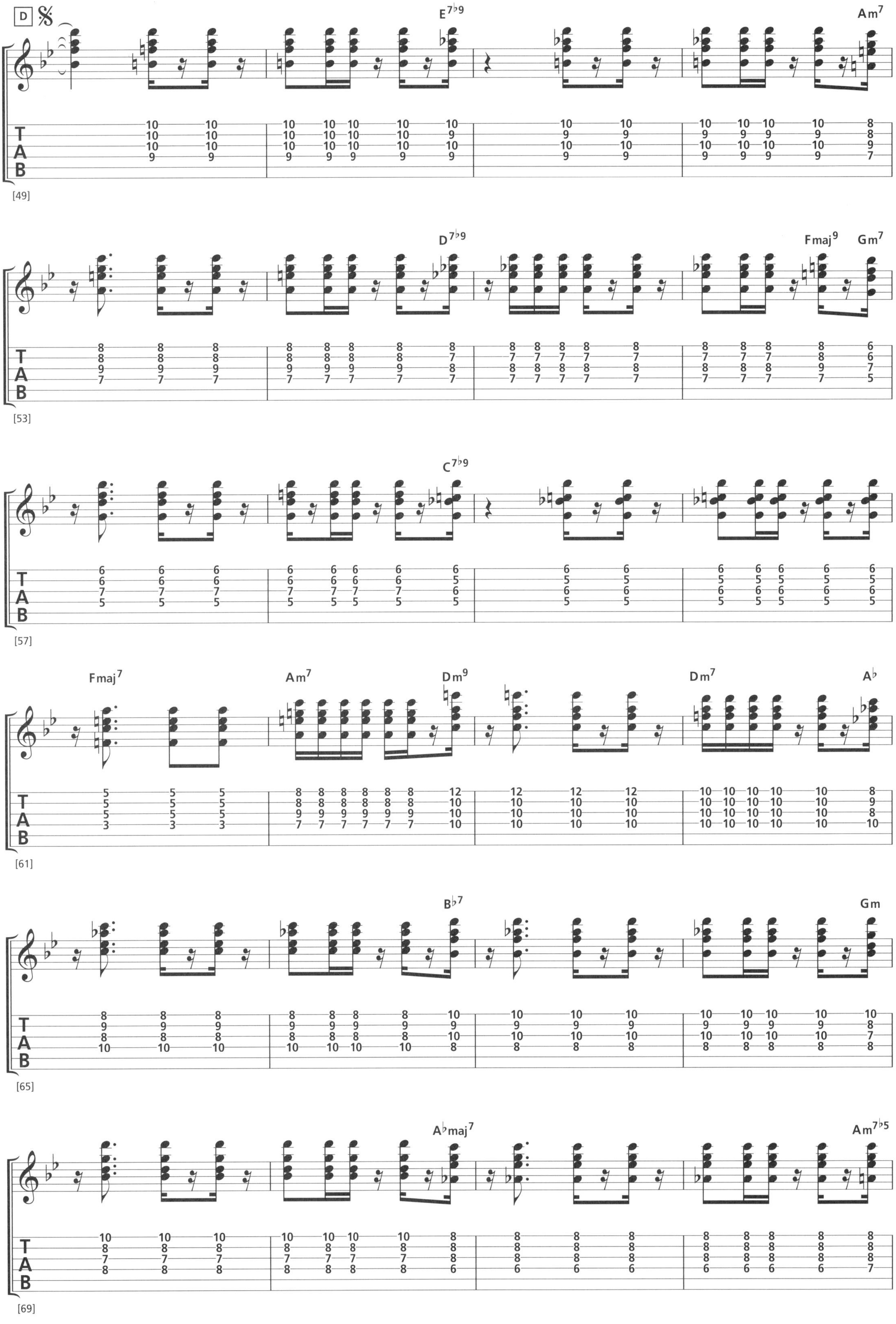
D
E7♭9
Am7
[49]
D7♭9
Fmaj9
Gm7
[53]
C7♭9
[57]
Fmaj7
Am7
Dm9
Dm7
A♭
[61]
B♭7
Gm
[65]
A♭maj7
Am7♭5
[69]

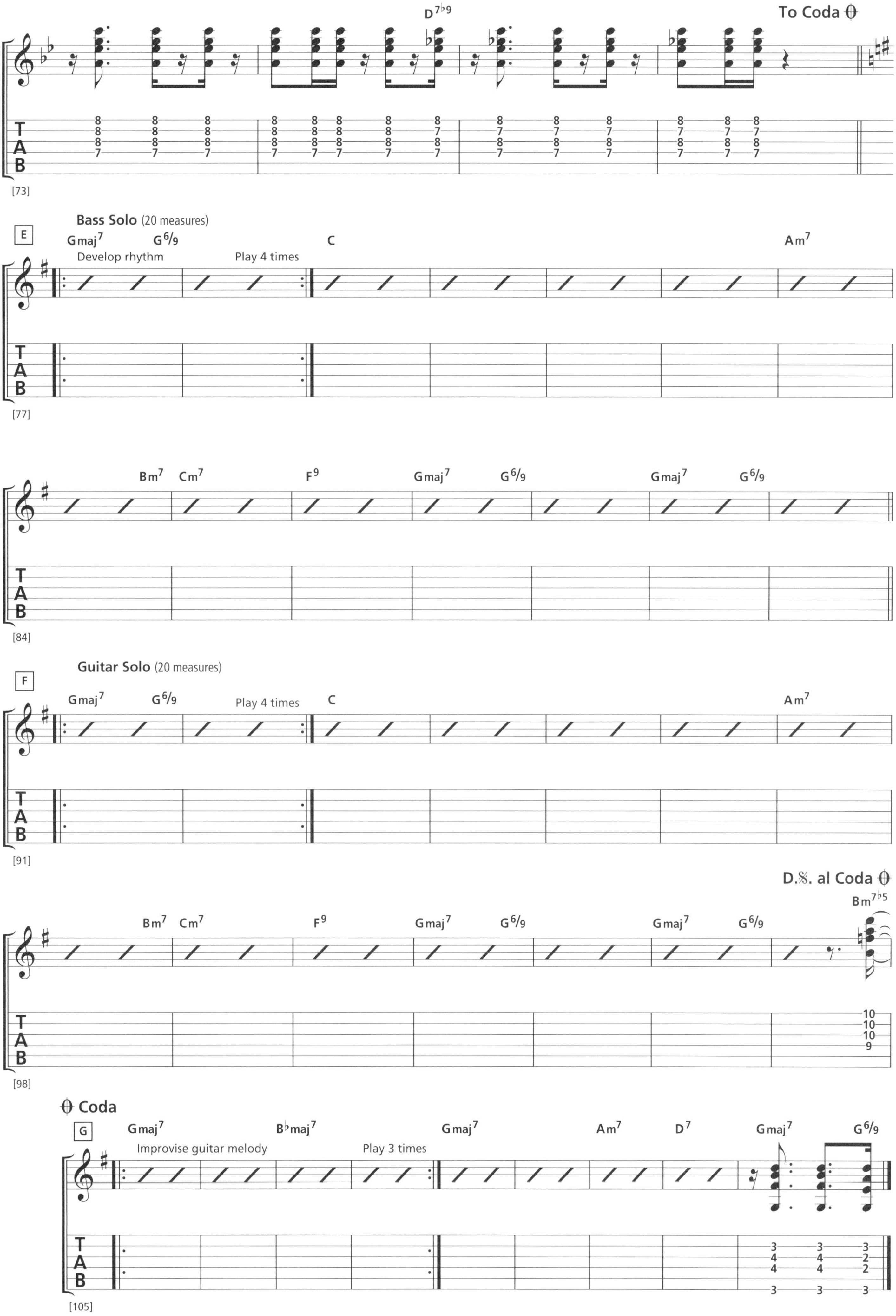

D7♭9
To Coda
[73]
Bass Solo (20 measures)
E
Gmaj7
G6/9
Develop rhythm
Play 4 times
C
Am7
[77]
Bm7
Cm7
F9
Gmaj7
G6/9
Gmaj7
G6/9
[84]
Guitar Solo (20 measures)
F
Gmaj7
G6/9
Play 4 times
C
Am7
[91]
D.%. al Coda
Bm7♭5
Bm7
Cm7
F9
Gmaj7
G6/9
Gmaj7
G6/9
[98]
Coda
G
Gmaj7
B♭maj7
Improvise guitar melody
Play 3 times
Gmaj7
Am7
D7
Gmaj7
G6/9
[105]

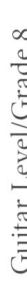

Walkthrough

Amp Settings

Aim for a clean tone that's full and warm. Using your guitar's neck pickup will help with this. Boost the bass (but don't let the sound become too muddy) and roll off the middle and treble if you feel the sound is too harsh. Reverb, if available, will greatly enhance the mood of this piece.

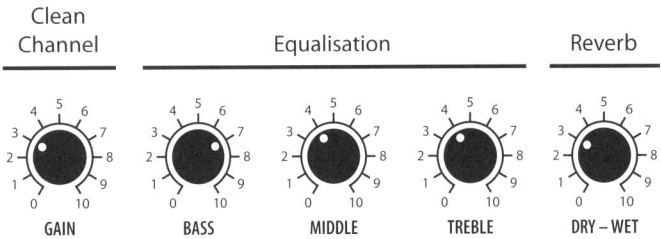

A & B sections (Measures 1–28)

The A & B sections are based on a fingerpicked chordal groove. The A section is a drum solo while the B section involves the bass playing the melody.

Measures 10-11 | *Cuíca*
The A section ends with an imitation of a cuíca, which is a high pitched sounding Brazilian drum. This unique sound is achieved by quickly sliding up from several frets below each note. This quick movement is challenging and you should ensure that the destination notes are played in time.

C Section (Measures 29–48)

The C section consists of an octave melody. Syncopated rhythms and fast position shifts make this a tricky section.

Measures 29-47 | *Sliding octaves*
Approach slides octaves in the same way as playing powerchords and barre chords: lock your fingers in position and move the fretting hand as a unit rather than dealing with individual finger placement.

D Section (Measures 49–76)

This intense rhythmic part uses, among others, several altered chords played on the first four strings of the guitar

Measures 49-76 | *Complex rhythms*
This rhythm will take some preparation to master. Work slowly while counting 16th notes ("1 e & a 2 e & a 3 e & a 4 e & a") (Fig. 1). Aim to 'feel' the rhythm rather than counting it to help your performance sound more convincing. A 16th note strumming pattern will help keep the pulse throughout the numerous syncopated rhythms.

E & F Sections (Measures 77–104)

The E section is the bass solo. The F section is a guitar solo.

Measures 77–90 | *Accompanying a solo*
While you must create an interesting part to accompany the bass solo, your primary goal is to support the soloist.

Measures 91–104 | *Guitar solo*
The G major scale will work throughout measures 91–98 and the C dorian mode for measures 99–100. Many jazz players opt for the lydian mode over the major scale because its ♯4 interval introduces tension that the major scale does not provide. If you wish to try this approach use G lydian in measures 91–92 and C lydian in measures 93–98.

G Section (Measures 105–113)

The G section is another opportunity for you to create you own part. This time, improvise a melody that complements the two-hand tapped part the bassist is playing.

Measures 105–113 | *G maj⁷ – B♭maj⁷ chord change*
Rather than changing scale position every time the chord changes (which may sound disjointed), stay in the same position and adjust the relevant notes every two measures. Start in G major then adjust the F♯, B and E to F♮, B♭ and E♭ respectively (Fig. 2).

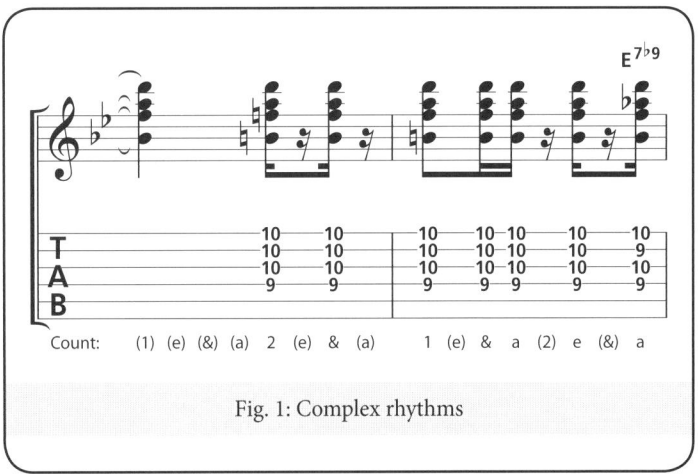

Fig. 1: Complex rhythms

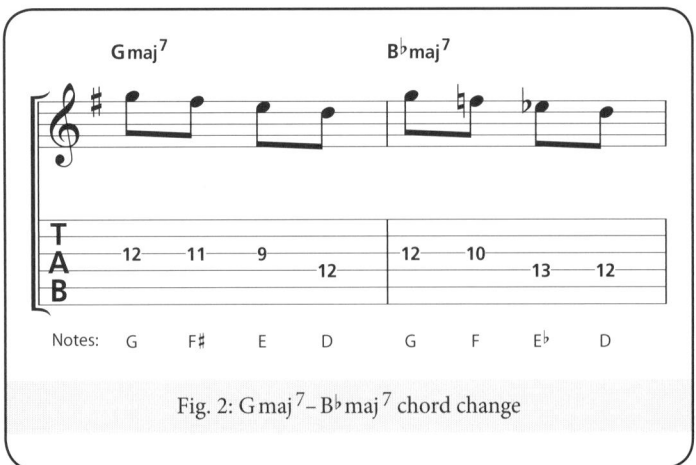

Fig. 2: G maj⁷ – B♭maj⁷ chord change

Dark Matter

SONG TITLE: DARK MATTER
GENRE: JAZZ
TEMPO: 121 BPM
KEY: A MINOR

TECH FEATURES: CHROMATICISM
FAST ALTERNATE PICKING
FUNK GROOVES

COMPOSERS: STUART RYAN, HENRY THOMAS & KUNG FU DRUMMER

PERSONNEL: STUART RYAN (GTR)
HENRY THOMAS (BASS)
NOAM LEDERMAN (DRUMS)
JAMES ARBURN (SAX)

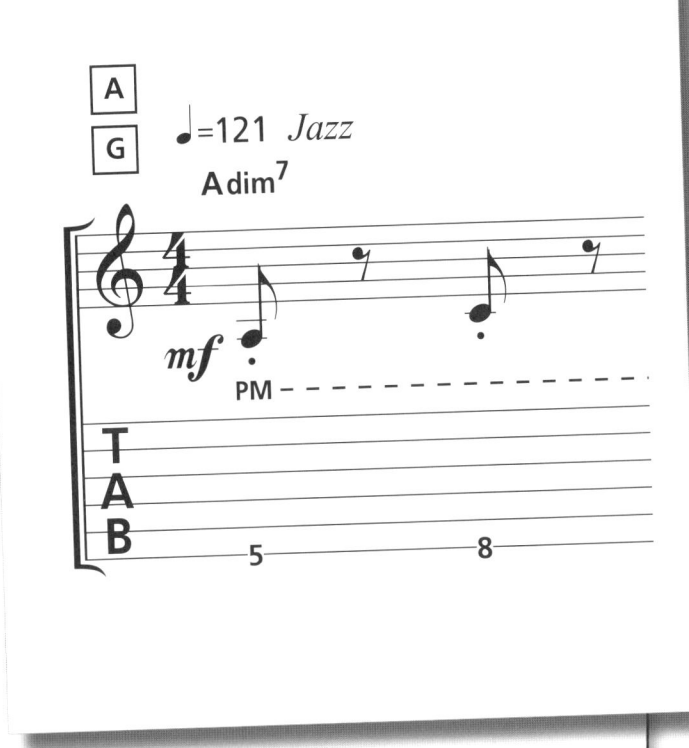

OVERVIEW

'Dark Matter' is a jazz funk piece in the style of Mike Stern and John Scofield. It features some challenging harmony interspersed with tight funk grooves. The melody is played as single notes, then with a darker sounding harmony. In keeping with this style there are chromatic ideas and displaced 16th note rhythms that require precise execution.

STYLE FOCUS

Jazz funk takes the harmony of jazz and combines it with the tight grooves of funk. Often a one-chord vamp will be used that allows the soloist to explore more complex scales and chromatic ideas. The chromatic runs in this piece offer a challenge to the picking hand and must be performed in time and with equal clarity to each note. In addition, this piece will test your timing and groove because you need to be able to play notes that are slightly displaced (i.e. not on the beat or offbeat but in between).

THE BIGGER PICTURE

Mike Stern and John Scofield came to prominence after performing with the legendary jazz trumpeter and pioneer of fusion Miles Davis. Both Stern and Scofield have a sophisticated grasp of jazz harmony and are able to employ dissonance in their music that often leads to a sense of tension and release.

Unlike traditional bebop guitarists, Stern and Scofield incorporated tones and ideas drawn from rock and funk to make their writing unpredictable. Chromaticism (using notes that don't necessarily belong in the given key) is widespread in their playing. This type of guitarist has great technical command of his instrument and is equally at home playing blistering lead lines or accompanying with sophisticated jazz-based chords.

RECOMMENDED LISTENING

Stern's 1988 album *Time In Place* showcases his great technique and the chromatic approach to writing that informs many of his melody lines. Scofield's *Groove Elation* (1995) is an accessible album that also boasts Hammond organ and brass in the line-up. *Still Warm* (1985) also takes the complex writing and harmony typical of his style. Another noteworthy jazz funk guitarist was the late Hiram Bullock. Similar to Prince's music of the early 1990s, Bullock's 1992 album *Way Kool* incorporated rhythms from the new jack swing genre popular at the time.

Dark Matter

Stuart Ryan, Henry Thomas & Kung Fu Drummer

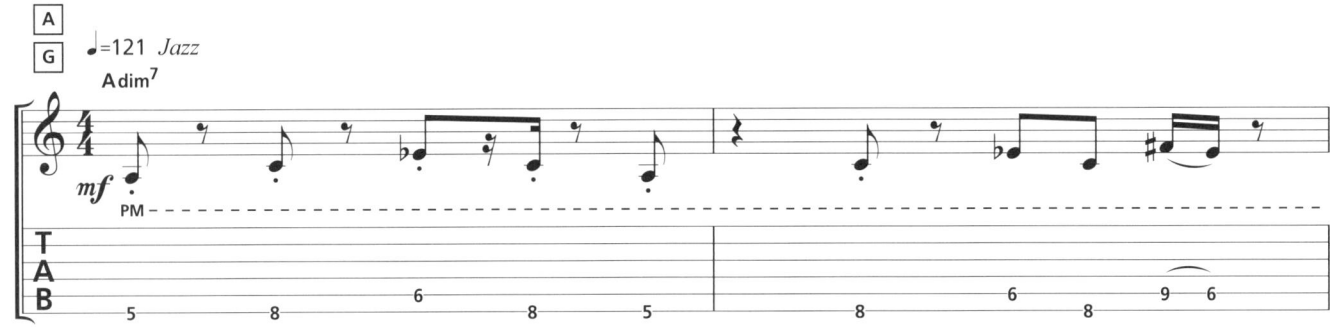
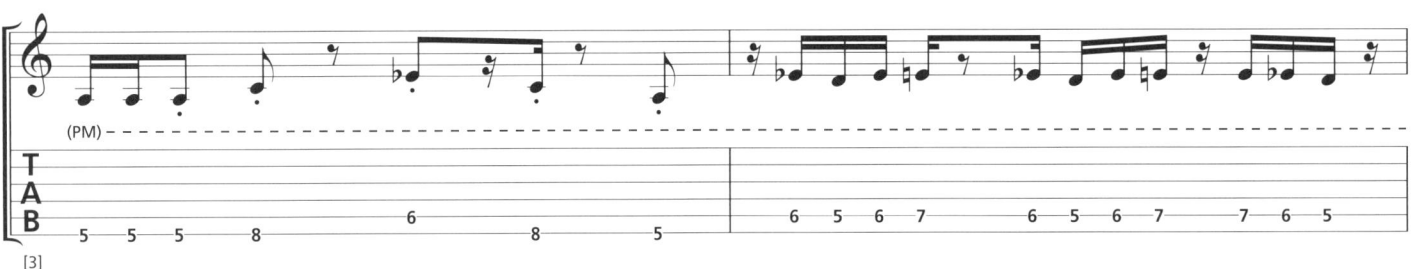
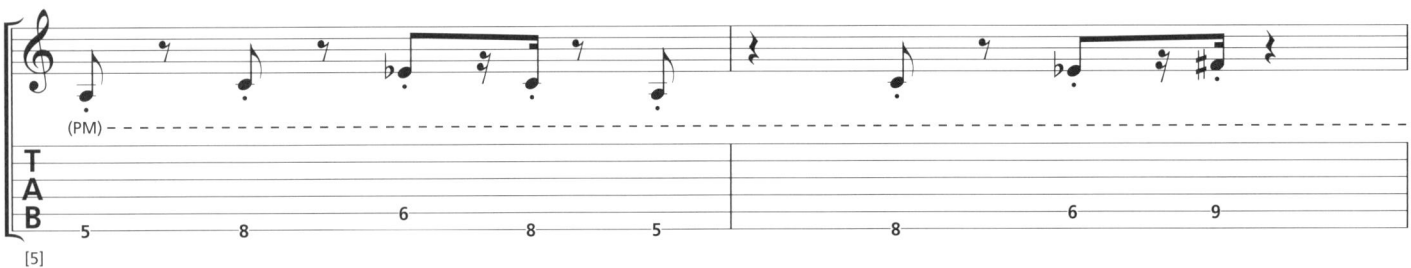
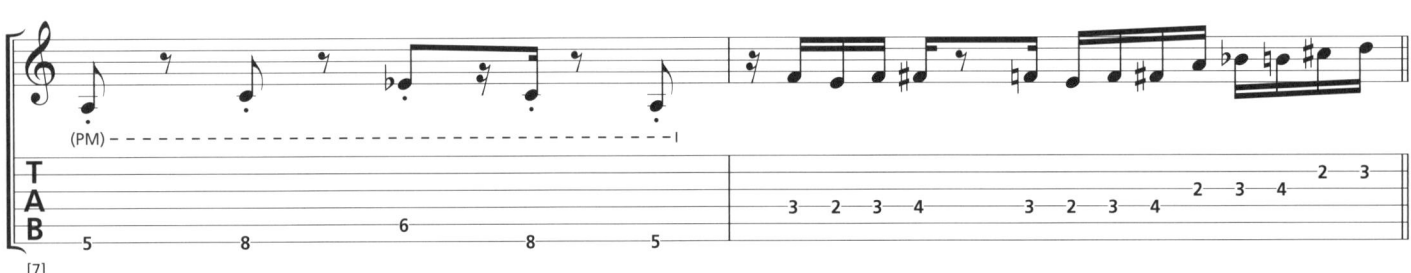

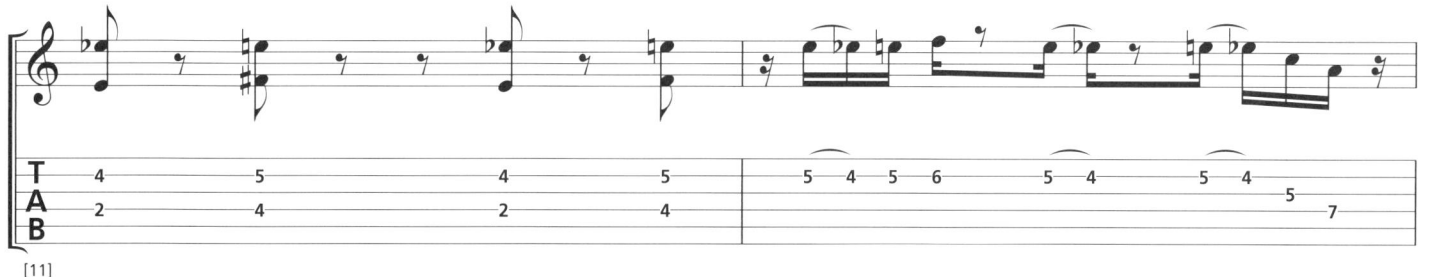
[11]

[13]

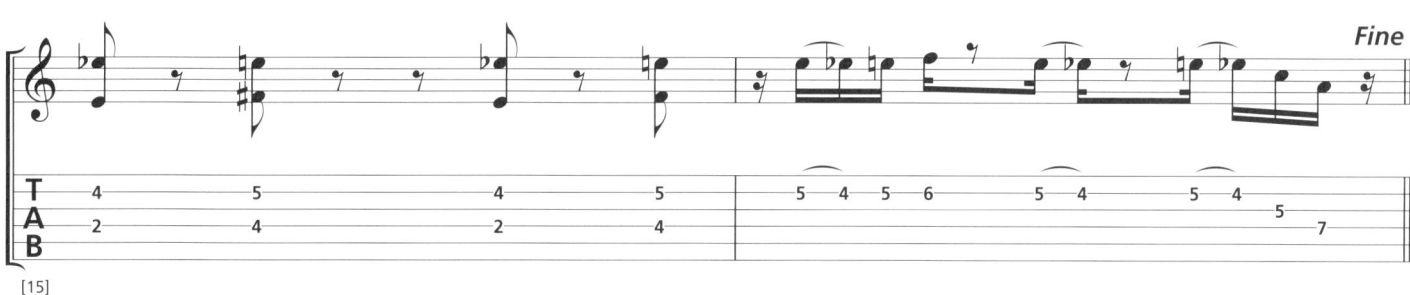
[15]

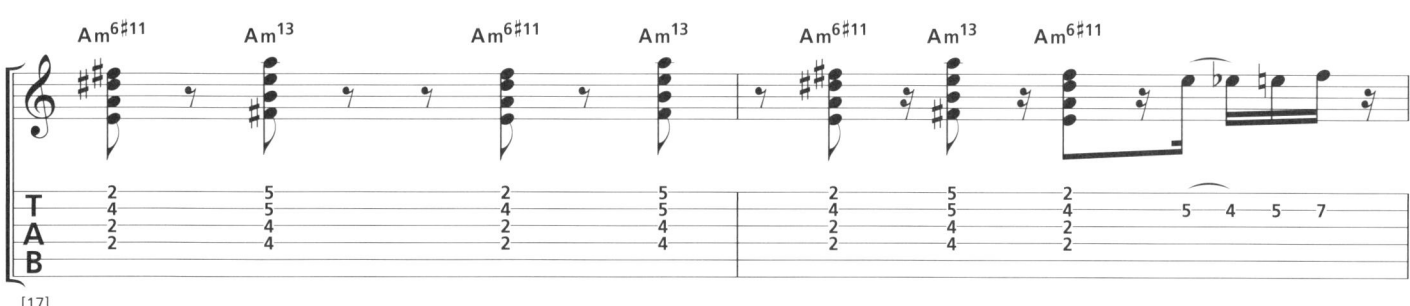
[17]

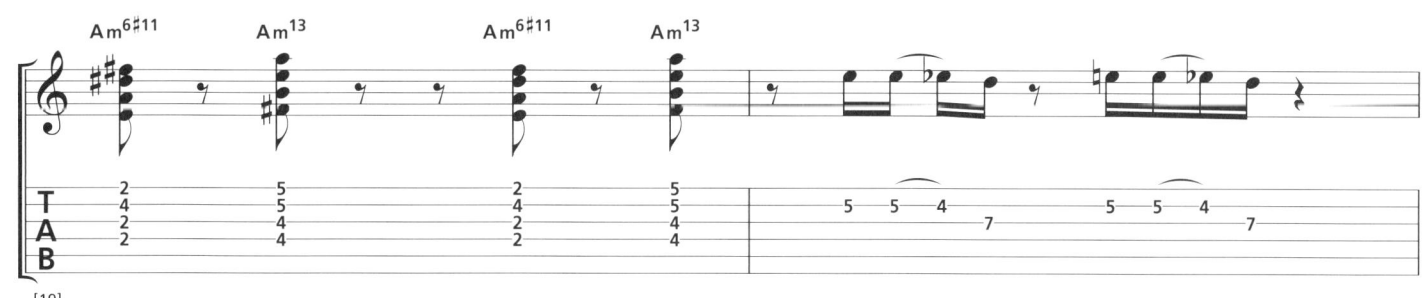
[19]

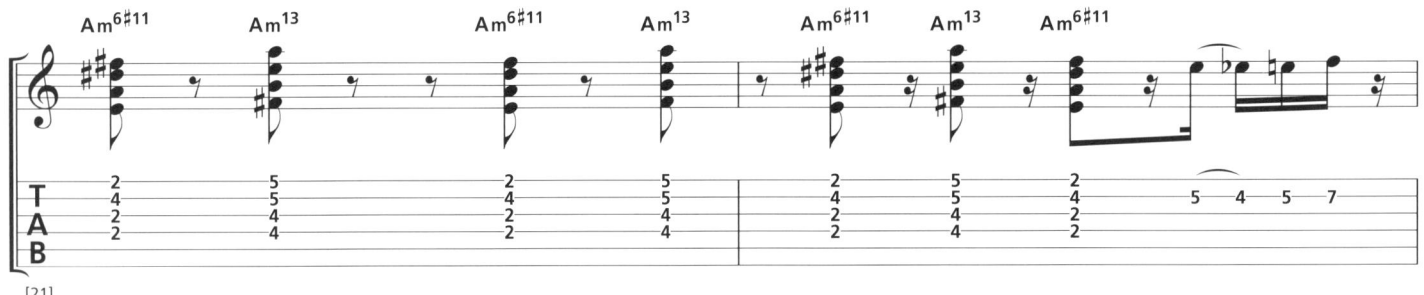
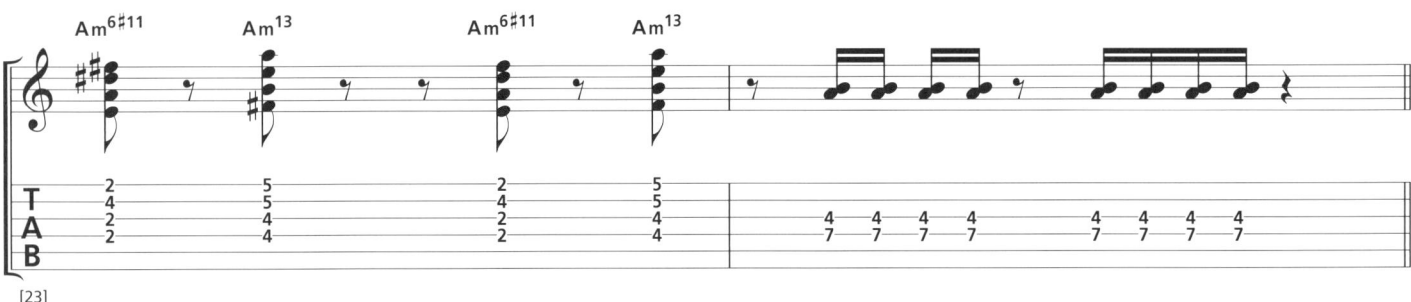
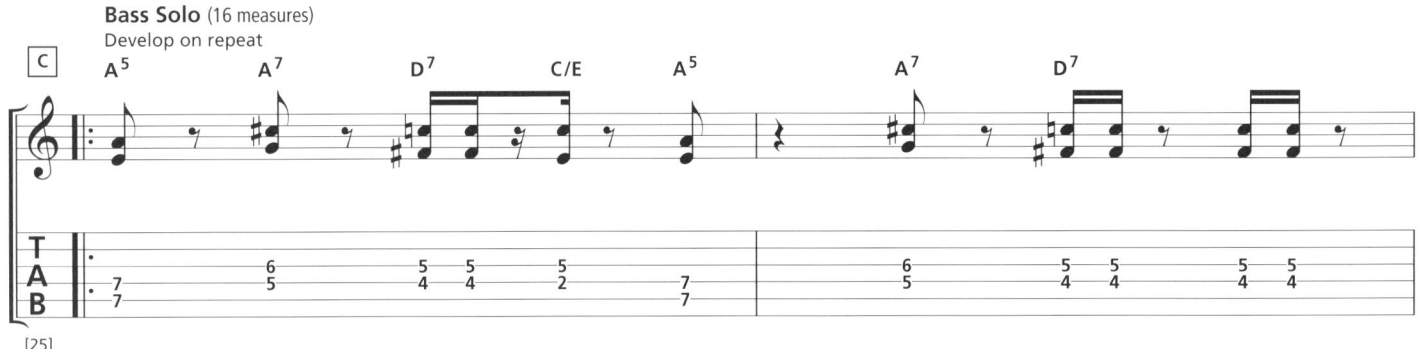
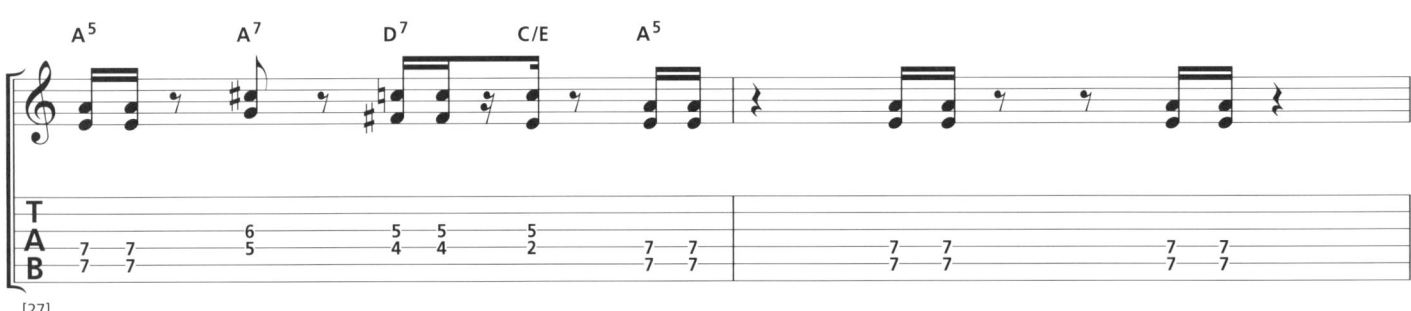
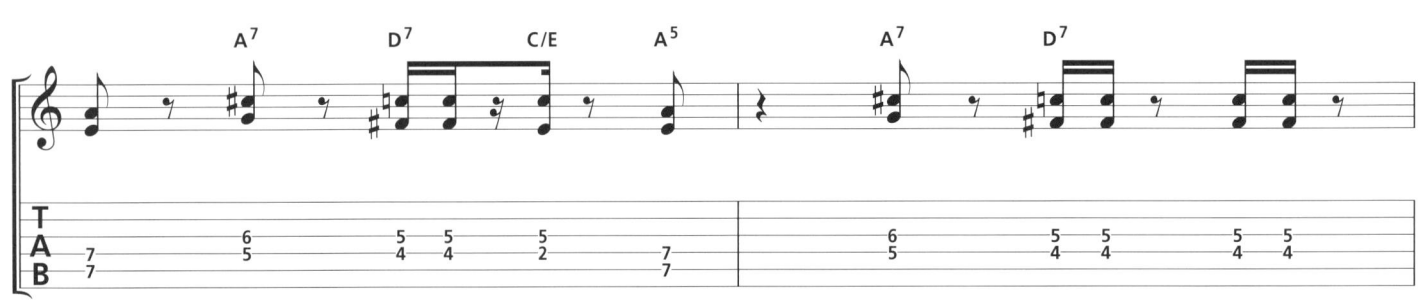

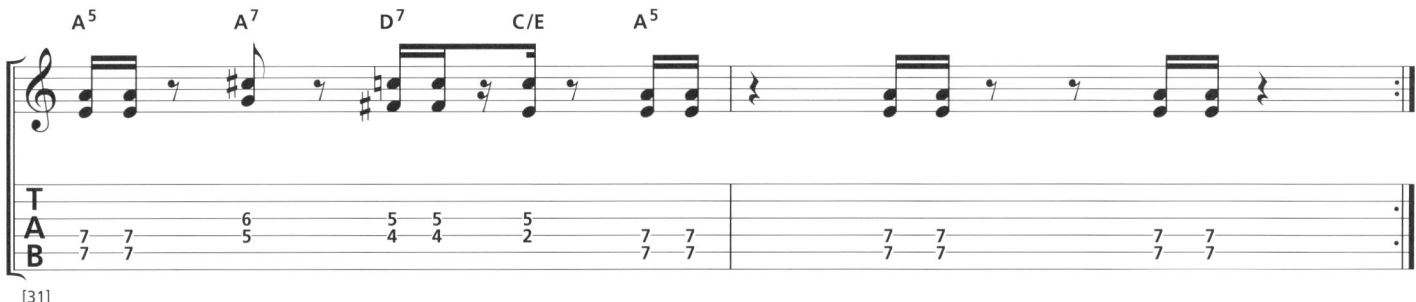
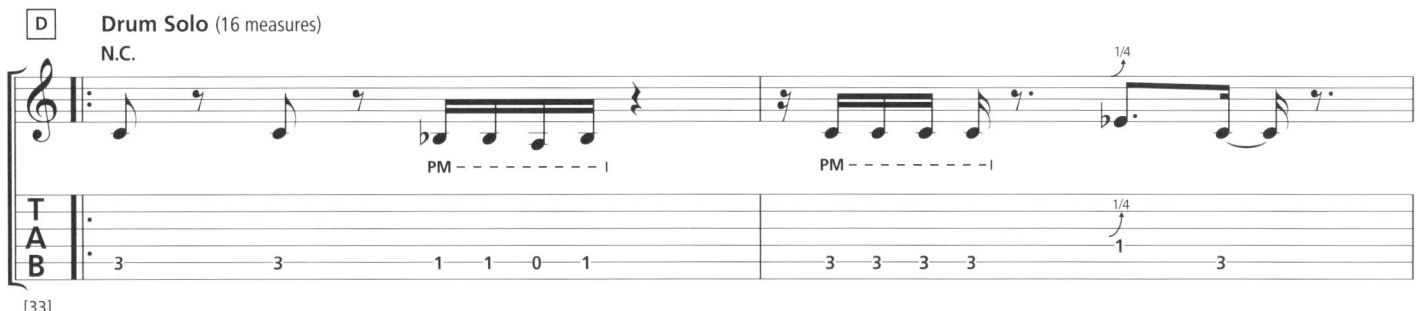
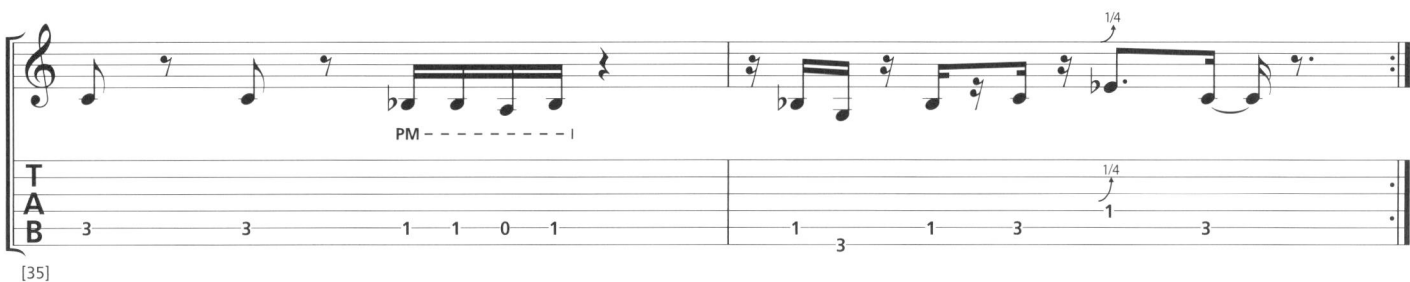
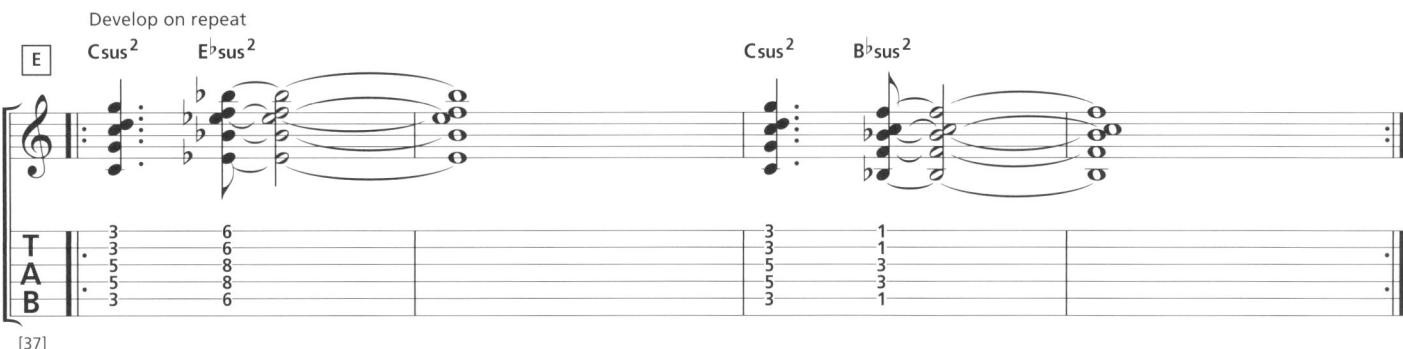
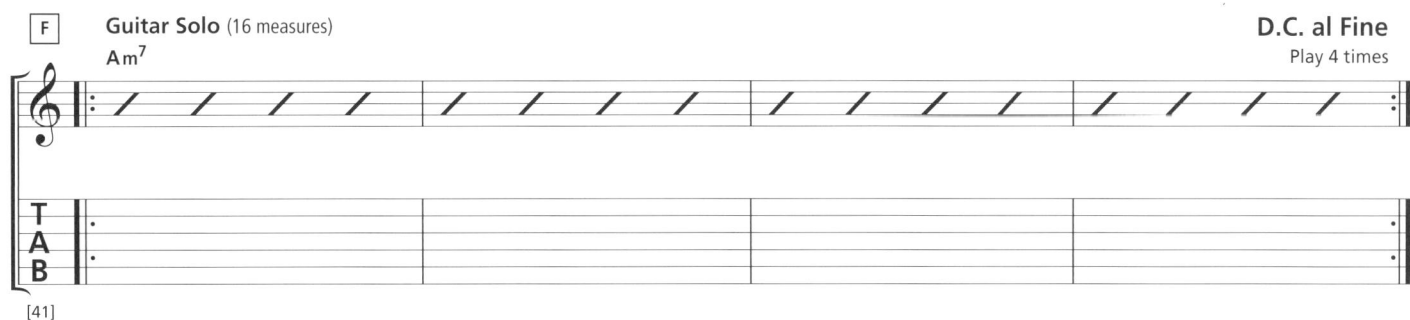

Walkthrough

Amp Settings
Use a clean tone for all of the sections apart from the solo where you may prefer to use a distorted sound. Aim for an overdriven sound with plenty of middle and a little reverb. A chorus pedal is often used in this style.

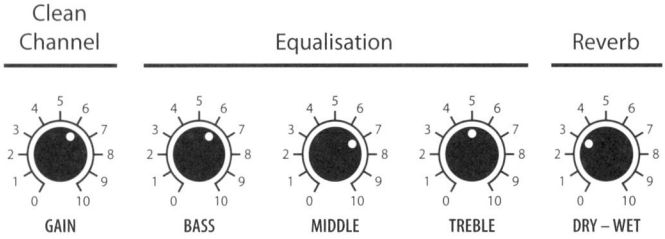

A & G Sections (Measures 1–8)
The A section is a heavily syncopated staccato riff based on an A diminished chord.

Measures 1–44 | *Syncopation*
There are many challenging syncopated parts in 'Dark Matter'. Most have distinctive grooves and should feel fairly natural. However, you may find that some require more in-depth study so break down each beat into 16th notes to see where each note falls.

Measure 4 | *Picking patterns*
While it usually feels natural to start phrases with a down stroke, the first two sequences in measure 4 start on the second and fourth 16th notes of their respective beats. Starting with an upstroke will place the down strokes on the stronger beats and give the phrase a more natural feel (Fig. 1).

B & H Sections (Measures 9–24)
The B section is also heavily syncopated and uses discordant major 7th intervals interspersed with bursts of 16th notes. This part is developed with the inclusion of four-note chords that contain the original major 7th intervals.

Measures 9–15 | *Major 7th intervals*
Make sure that you play the notated major 7th intervals, which can easily be mistaken for octaves (Fig. 2).

C Section (Measures 25–32)
The C section is the bass solo accompanied by the guitar playing funky diads. You have the opportunity to develop this part on the repeat.

Measures 25–32 | *Note lengths*
Correct note lengths are key to the feel of this tight, funky riff. Ensure the notes are allowed to ring on. Listen to the recording and really lock in with the bass and drums.

D & E Sections (Measures 33–40)
The D section is the drum solo accompanied by another single-note riff. The E section is a chordal part that uses suspended chords and, once again, you have the opportunity to develop the part on the repeat.

Measures 37–40 | *Develop on repeat*
When you develop a part be faithful to the original notation while still taking the section somewhere new. Common ways to develop a part are to vary the rhythm or use different chord voicings. These are, of course, only suggestions and you should play the part as you feel works best.

F Section (Measures 41–44)
The F section is a 16-measure guitar solo and is based in A minor. The single chord vamp is an excellent opportunity to explore more adventurous scale choices.

Measures 41–44 | *Guitar solo*
Although the guitar solo is based on a single Am^7 chord, simply using the blues or minor pentatonic scale is unlikely to yield a stylistically convincing result. Fusion guitarists are well-known for their use of exotic scales and arpeggios as well as a large amount of chromaticism. Experiment with different scale choices to increase your options for this solo. The dorian and phrygian modes are a good place to start.

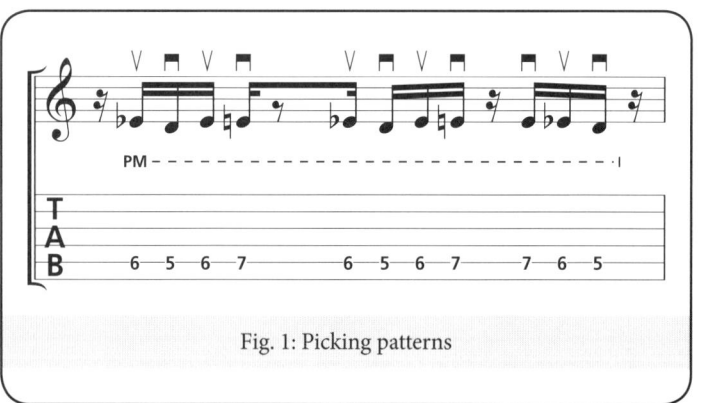

Fig. 1: Picking patterns

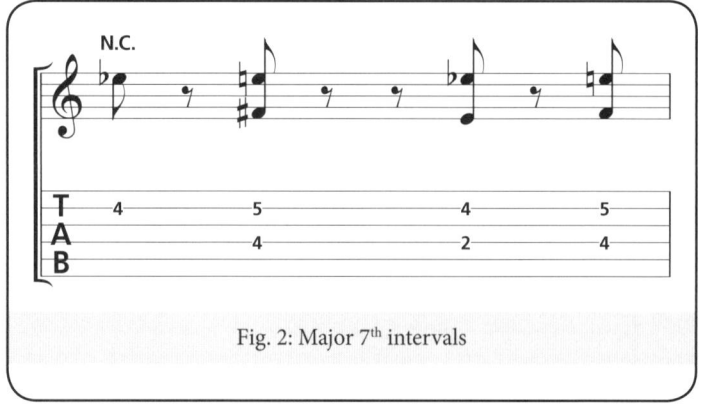

Fig. 2: Major 7th intervals

Technical Exercises

In this section the assessor will ask you to play a selection of exercises drawn from each of the four groups shown below. Groups A, B and C contain examples of the scales and modes, arpeggios and chords you can use when playing the pieces. In Group D you will be asked to prepare *one* stylistic study from the three printed. Your choice of stylistic study will determine the style of the Quick Study Piece.

You do not need to memorise the exercises (and can use the book in the assessment) but the assessor will be looking for the speed of your response. The assessor will also give credit for the level of your musicality.

Before you start the section you will be asked whether you would like to play the exercises along with the click or hear a single measure of click before you commence the test. The tempo is ♩ = 100.

Group A: Scales
Two octaves, two positions. The first position is to be prepared on the E string from the starting notes of G–B chromatically. The second position is to be prepared on the A string from the starting notes of C–E chromatically.

1. Whole tone (G whole tone shown, root on E string)

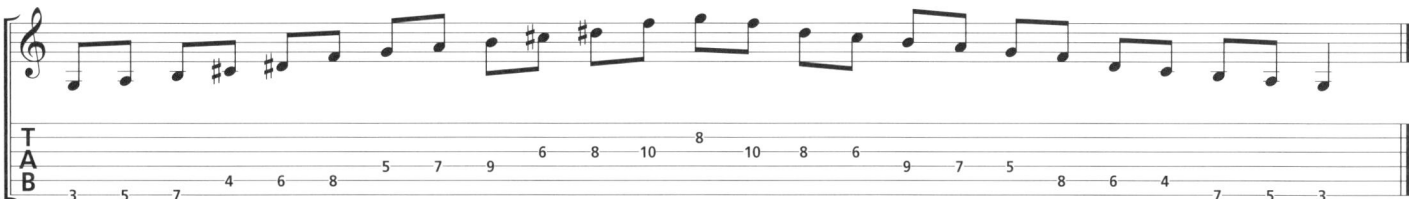

2. Diminished (D diminished shown, root on A string)

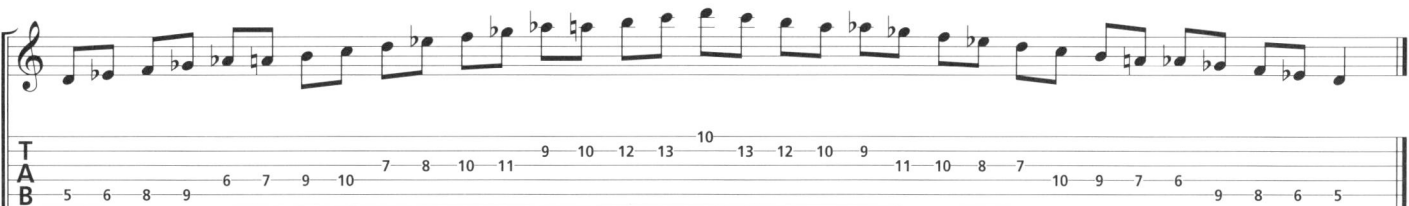

3. Altered (C altered shown, root on A string)

Technical Exercises

Group B: Arpeggios

One octave, two positions. The first position is to be prepared on the E string from the starting notes of G–B chromatically. The second position is to be prepared on the A string from the starting notes of C–E chromatically.

1. Dominant$^{7\sharp 5}$ arpeggios (G$^{7\sharp 5}$ arpeggio shown, root on E string)

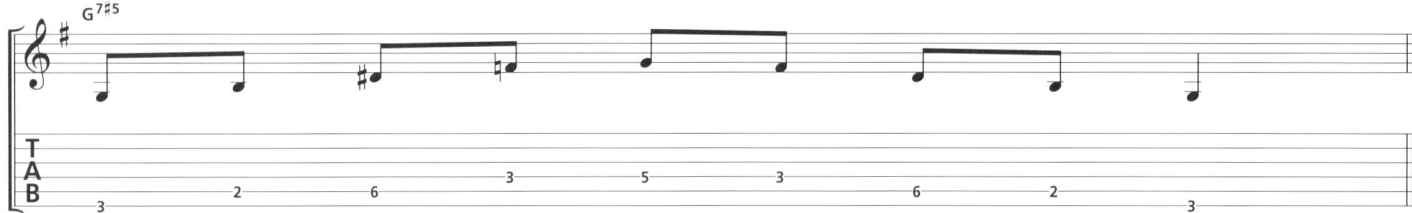

2. Dominant$^{7\flat 5}$ arpeggios (A$^{7\flat 5}$ arpeggio shown, root on E string)

3. Minor$^{7\flat 5}$ arpeggios (Cm$^{7\flat 5}$ arpeggio shown, root on A string)

4. Dominant$^{7\sharp 9}$ arpeggios (D$^{7\sharp 9}$ arpeggio shown, root on A string)

5. Dominant$^{7\flat 9}$ arpeggios (E$^{7\flat 9}$ arpeggio shown, root on A string)

6. Diminished arpeggios (A diminished arpeggio shown, root on E string)

Technical Exercises

Group C: Chords

To be prepared in two positions. The first position is to be prepared on the E string from the starting notes of G–B chromatically. The second position is to be prepared on the A string from the starting notes of C–E chromatically. Chords should be strummed and then picked (arpeggiated).

1. Dominant $7{\sharp}5$ (G$^{7{\sharp}5}$ chord shown, root on E string)

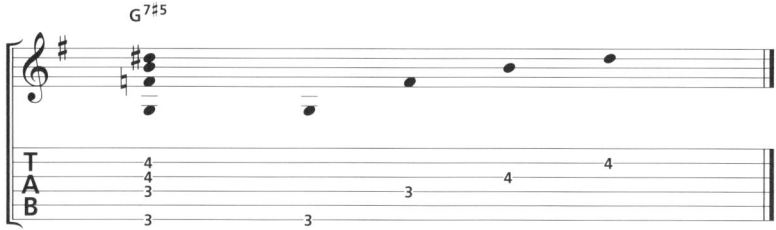

2. Dominant $7{\flat}5$ (A$^{7{\flat}5}$ chord shown, root on E string)

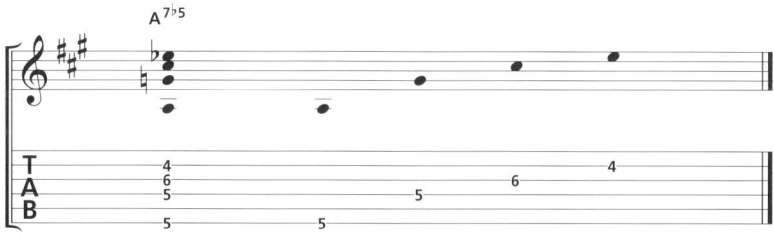

3. Dominant $7{\sharp}9$ (D$^{7{\sharp}9}$ arpeggio shown, root on A string)

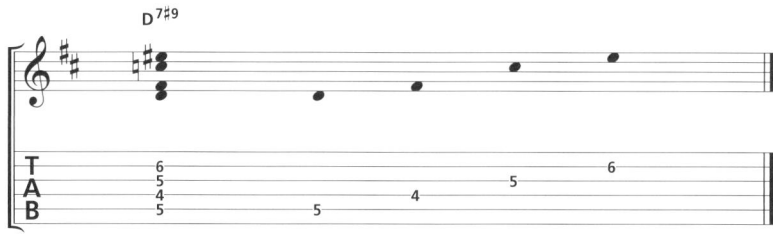

4. Dominant $7{\flat}9$ (E$^{7{\flat}9}$ arpeggio shown, root on A string)

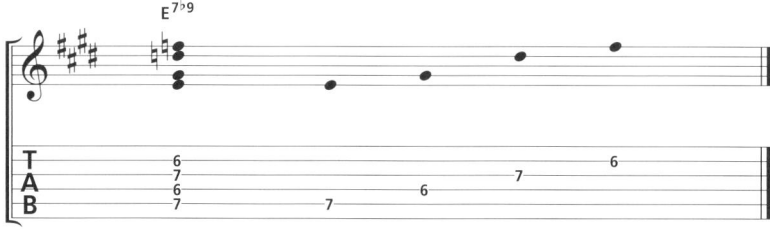

Technical Exercises

Group D: Stylistic Studies

You will prepare a technical study from one group of styles from the list below. Your choice of style will determine the style of the Quick Study Piece.

1. Rock/Metal: crossing strings and alternate picking

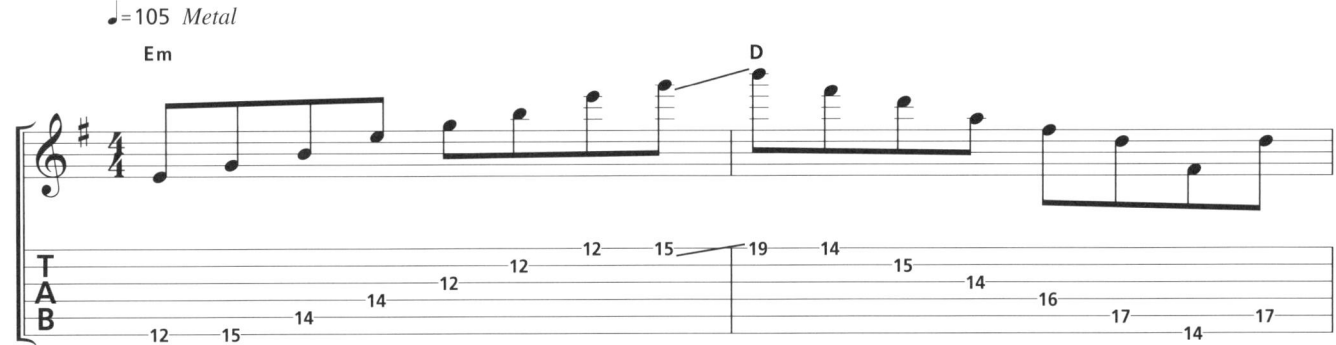
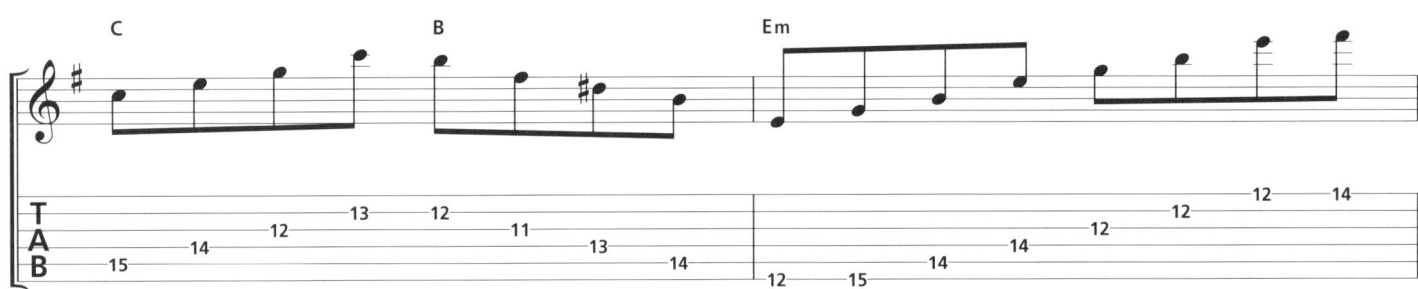
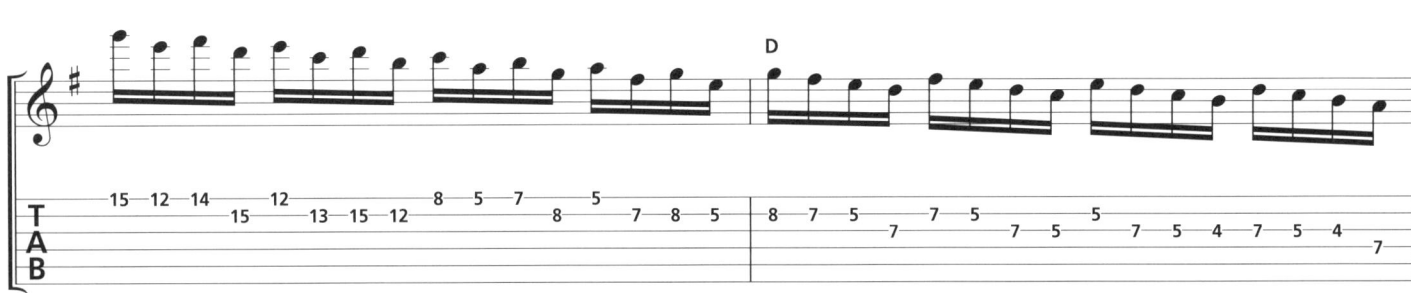

Technical Exercises

2. Funk: chordal embellishments and muted strings

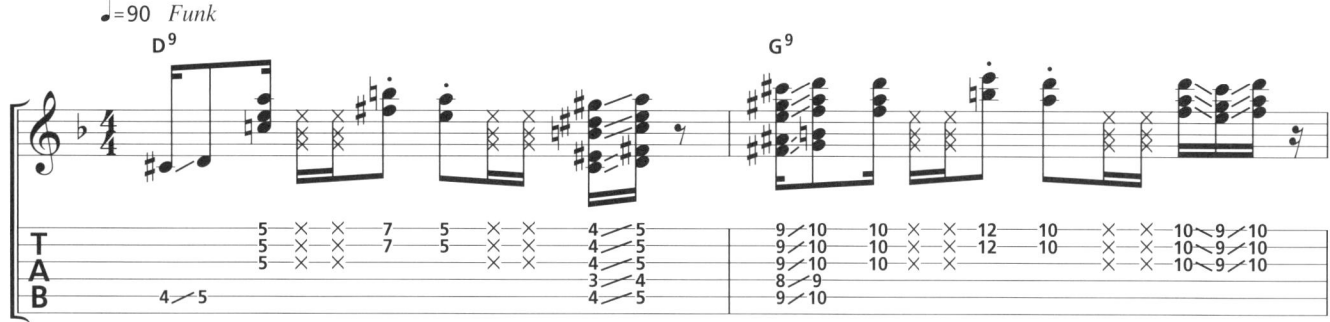

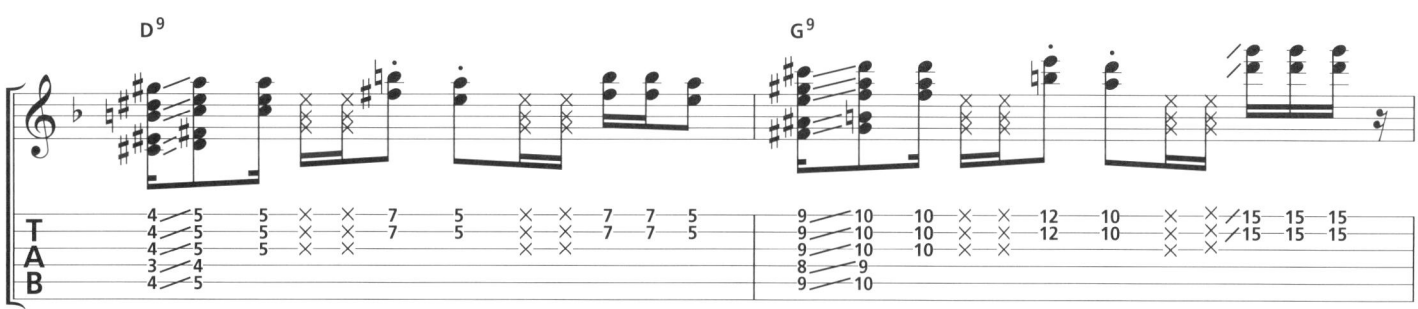

Technical Exercises

3. Jazz/Latin/Blues: legato phrasing and alternate picking

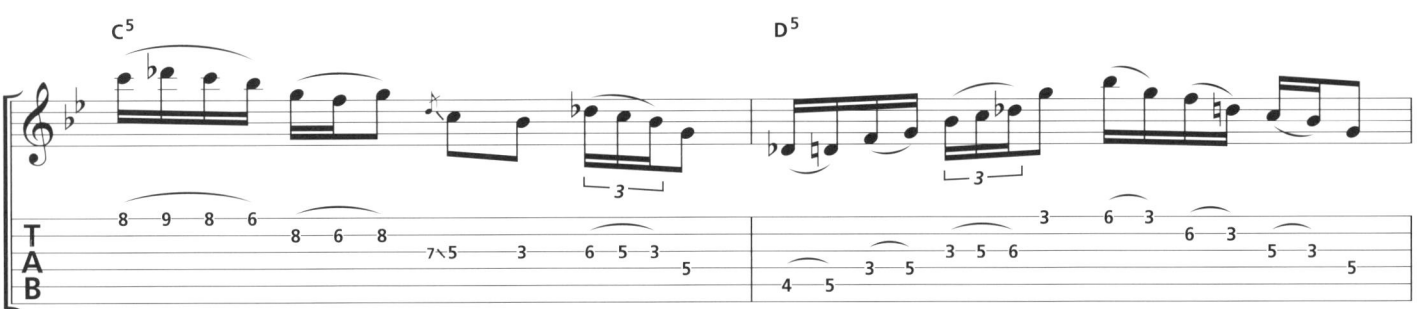

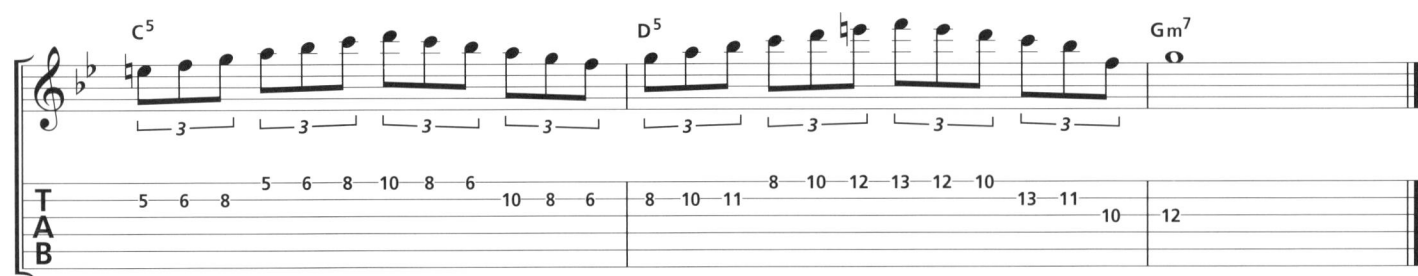

Quick Study Piece

At this level/grade, you will be asked to prepare and play a short Quick Study Piece (QSP). Printed below are three examples of the type of QSP you are likely to receive in the assessment. You will be shown the test and played the track with the *notated parts played*. Any measures that require improvisation will not be demonstrated. You will then have three minutes to study the test. The backing track will be played twice more. You will be allowed to practise during the first playing of the backing track, with the notated parts now absent, before playing it to the assessor on the second playing of the backing track.

The style of your QSP is determined by the stylistic study you selected in the technical exercise section. The QSP is in the form of a lead sheet and it is up to you to create your own interpretation of the music in the parts marked for improvisation.

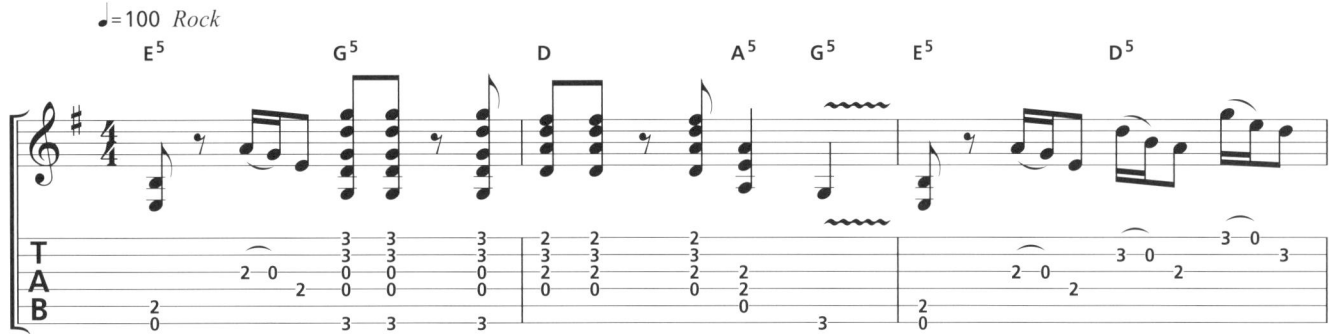

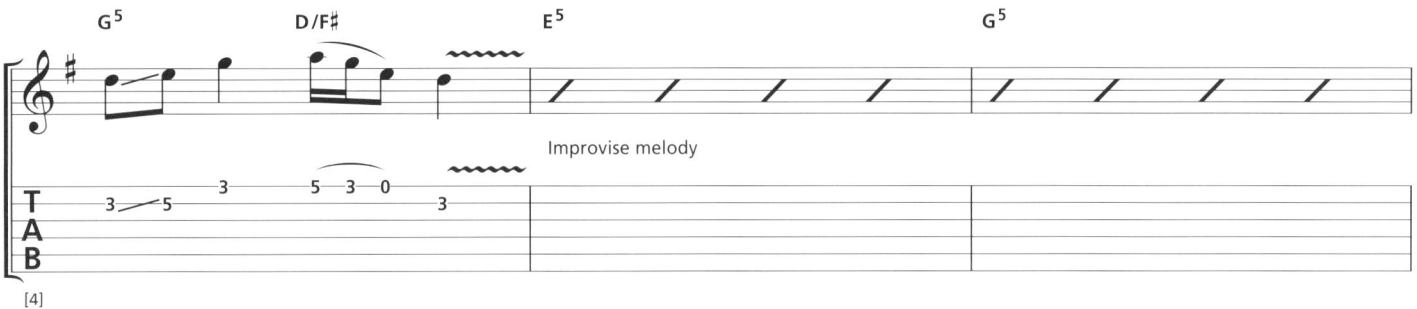

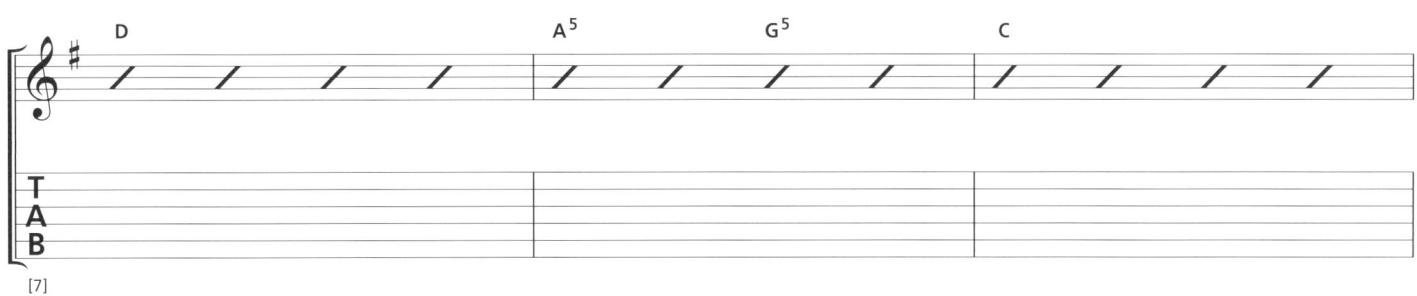

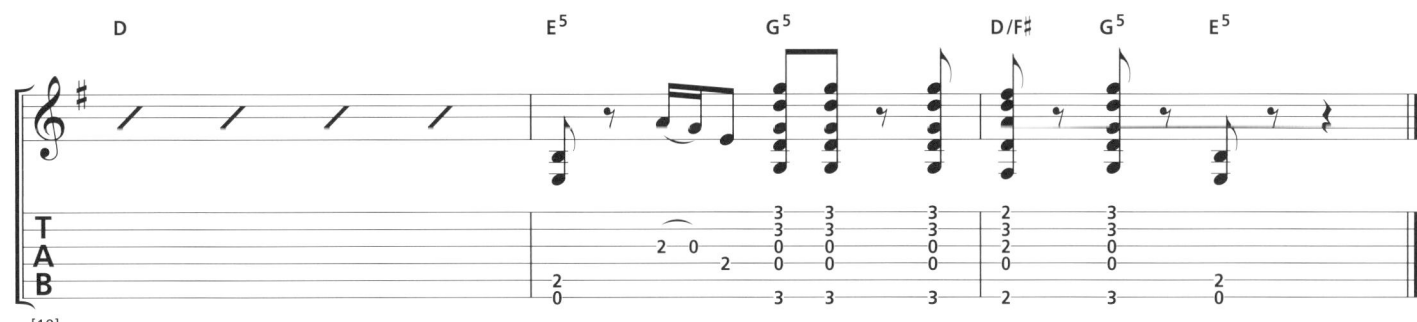

Quick Study Piece

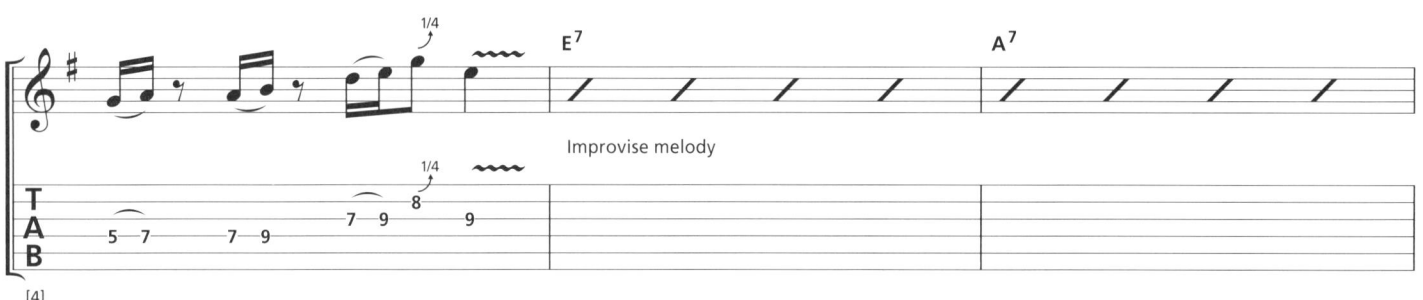
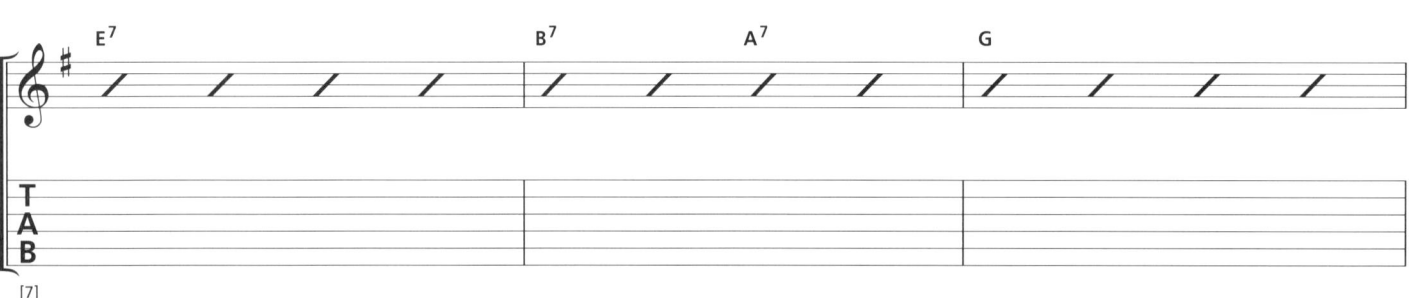
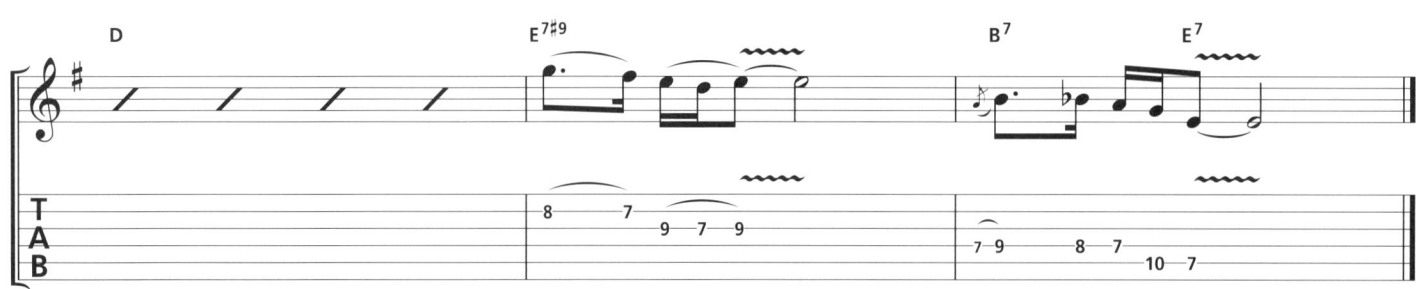

Quick Study Piece

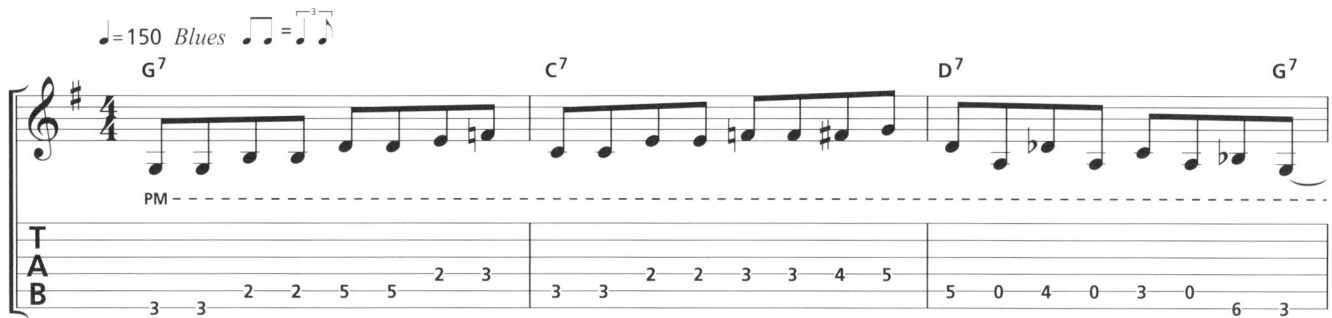
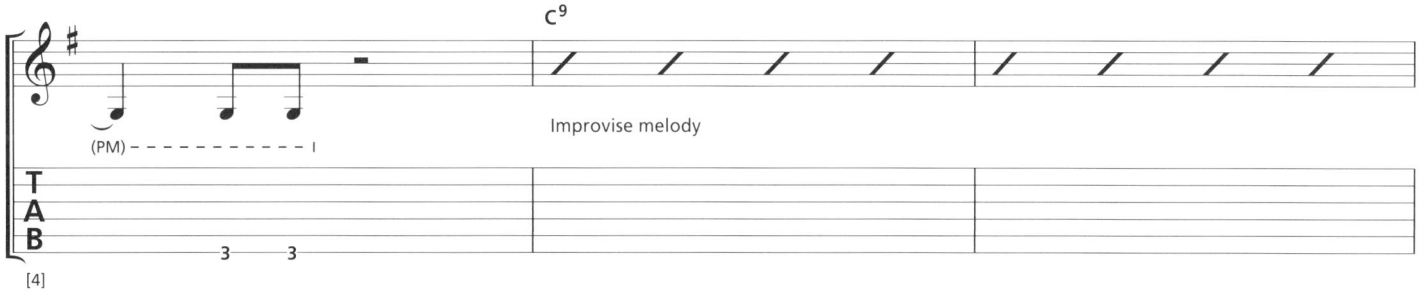
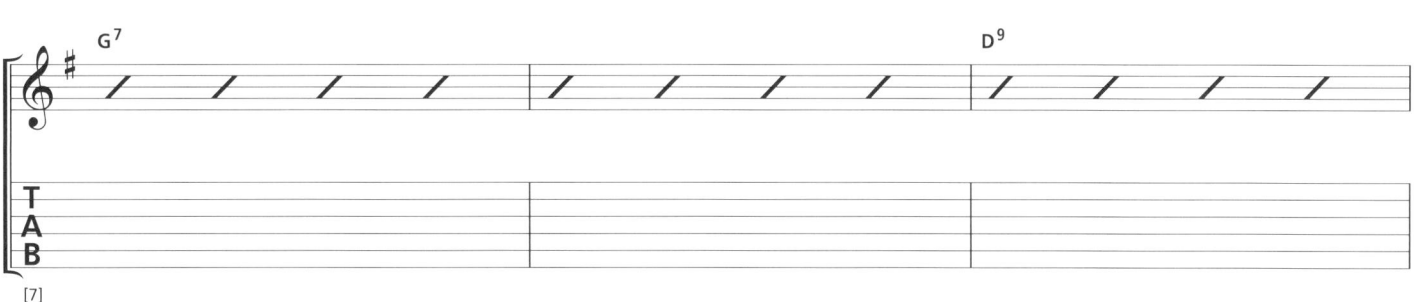
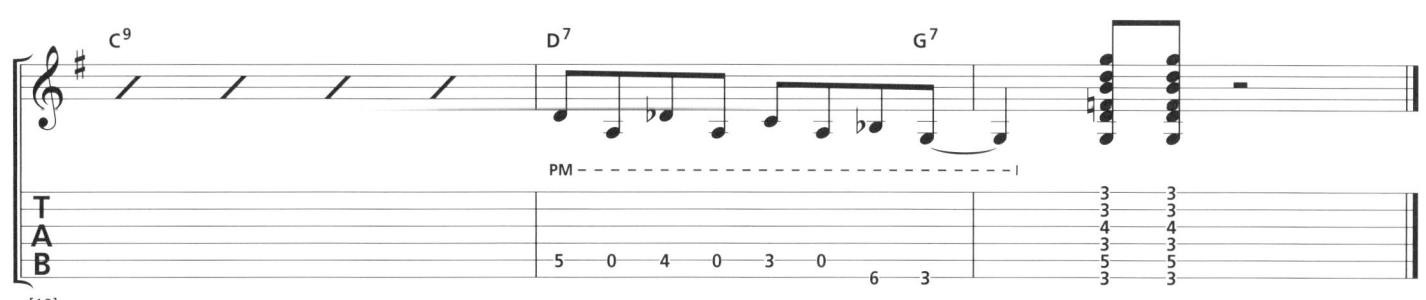

Ear Tests

There are two Ear Tests in this level/grade. The assessor will play each test to you twice. You will find one example of each type of test printed below.

Test 1: Melodic Recall
The assessor will play you a two-measure melody with a bass and drum backing using either the E major pentatonic, F minor pentatonic or B natural minor scales. The first note of the melody will be *either* the root note, third *or* fifth and the first interval will be *either* ascending *or* descending. You will play the melody back on your instrument. You will hear the test twice.

Each time the test is played the sequence is: count-in, root note, count-in, melody. There will be a short gap for you to practise after you have heard the test for the second time. You will hear the count-in and root note for the third time followed by a *vocal* count-in and you will then play the melody to the bass and drum backing. The tempo is ♩=90.

Test 2: Harmonic Recall
The assessor will play you a tonic chord followed by a four-measure chord sequence in the key of E major played to a bass and drum backing. The sequence will use the I, ii, iii, IV, V and vi chords. The I and IV chords can be either major or major⁷ chords. You will be asked to play the chord sequence to the bass and drum backing in the rhythm show in the example below. This rhythm will be used in all examples of this test given in the assessment. You will then be asked to identify the sequence you have played to the assessor, including any chord extensions. You will hear the test twice.

Each time the test is played the sequence is: count-in, tonic, count-in, chords. There will be a short gap for you to practise after you have heard the test for the second time. You will hear the count-in and tonic for the third time followed by a *vocal* count-in and you will then play the chords to the bass and drum backing. You should then name the chords, including any extensions. The tempo is ♩=90.

General Musicianship Questions

In this part of the assessment you will be asked five questions. Four of these questions will be about general music knowledge and the fifth question asked will be about your instrument.

Music Knowledge

The assessor will ask you four music knowledge questions based on a piece of music that you have played in the assessment. You will nominate the piece of music about which the questions will be asked. In this level/grade, you will be asked to identify and demonstrate your answers on your instrument as directed by the assessor.

In Level/Grade 8 you will be asked to explain:

- The names of pitches

- Any expressive musical marking found in the piece such as palm muting, accents, staccato, legato, vibrato, natural and artificial harmonics

- Any dynamic marking found in the piece

- The types of scale that can be used appropriately in the solo section of the piece you have played and its relation to the underlying harmony of the piece

Instrument Knowledge

The assessor will also ask you one question regarding your instrument.

In Level/Grade 8 you will be asked to explain and demonstrate:

- Where to find the same pitch on two different strings

- The function of the volume and tone controls on your guitar

- The set up for the tone required for the piece you have played on the amp

- How to achieve changes in tone in a song

Further Information

Tips on how to approach this part of this assessment can be found in the *Syllabus Guide* for guitar, the Rockschool *Guitar Companion Guide* and on the Rockschool website: *www.rslawards.com*. The Introduction to Tone, a comprehensive explanation of guitar tones, can be found at the back of each level/grade book and the tone guide to each piece is in the appropriate Walkthrough.

Entering Rockschool Assessments

Entering a Rockschool assessment is easy, just go online and follow our simple six step process. All details for entering online, dates, fees, regulations and Free Choice pieces can be found at *www.rslawards.com*

- All candidates should ensure they bring their own Level/Grade syllabus book to the assessment or have proof of digital purchase ready to show the assessor.

- All Level/Grade 6–8 candidates must ensure that they bring valid photo ID to their assessment.

Marking Schemes

DEBUT TO LEVEL/GRADE 5 *

ELEMENT	PASS	MERIT	DISTINCTION
Performance Piece 1	12–14 out of 20	15–17 out of 20	18+ out of 20
Performance Piece 2	12–14 out of 20	15–17 out of 20	18+ out of 20
Performance Piece 3	12–14 out of 20	15–17 out of 20	18+ out of 20
Technical Exercises	9–10 out of 15	11–12 out of 15	13+ out of 15
Sight Reading *or* Improvisation & Interpretation	6 out of 10	7–8 out of 10	9+ out of 10
Ear Tests	6 out of 10	7–8 out of 10	9+ out of 10
General Musicianship Questions	3 out of 5	4 out of 5	5 out of 5
TOTAL MARKS	60%+	74%+	90%+

LEVELS/GRADES 6–8

ELEMENT	PASS	MERIT	DISTINCTION
Performance Piece 1	12–14 out of 20	15–17 out of 20	18+ out of 20
Performance Piece 2	12–14 out of 20	15–17 out of 20	18+ out of 20
Performance Piece 3	12–14 out of 20	15–17 out of 20	18+ out of 20
Technical Exercises	9–10 out of 15	11–12 out of 15	13+ out of 15
Quick Study Piece	6 out of 10	7–8 out of 10	9+ out of 10
Ear Tests	6 out of 10	7–8 out of 10	9+ out of 10
General Musicianship Questions	3 out of 5	4 out of 5	5 out of 5
TOTAL MARKS	60%+	74%+	90%+

PERFORMANCE CERTIFICATES | DEBUT TO LEVEL/GRADE 8 *

ELEMENT	PASS	MERIT	DISTINCTION
Performance Piece 1	12–14 out of 20	15–17 out of 20	18+ out of 20
Performance Piece 2	12–14 out of 20	15–17 out of 20	18+ out of 20
Performance Piece 3	12–14 out of 20	15–17 out of 20	18+ out of 20
Performance Piece 4	12–14 out of 20	15–17 out of 20	18+ out of 20
Performance Piece 5	12–14 out of 20	15–17 out of 20	18+ out of 20
TOTAL MARKS	60%+	75%+	90%+

* Note that there are no Debut Vocal assessments.

Introduction to Tone

A large part of an effective guitar performance is selecting the right tone. The electric guitar's sound is subject to a wide range of variables, and this guide outlines the basic controls present on most amplifiers as well as the common variations between models. There is also a basic overview of pickups and the effect their location on the guitar has on tone. Finally, it covers the differences between the types of distortion, which is crucial to getting your basic sound right.

At Level/Grade 8, the tone may change within the course of a piece. You should aim to use a tone that is stylistically appropriate and you may bring your own equipment to the assessment room for this purpose. There is a tone guide at the start of each Walkthrough to help you.

Basic amplifier controls

Most amplifiers come with a standard set of controls that are the same as, or very similar to, the diagram below. It's important to understand what each control is and the effect that it has on your guitar's tone.

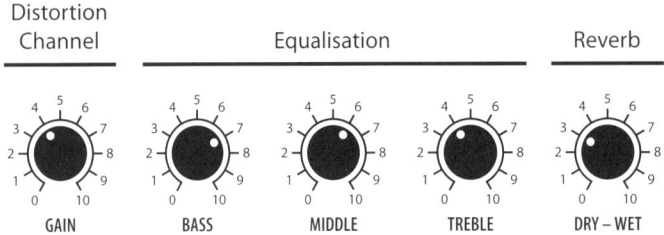

- **Channel (Clean/Distortion)**
  Most amplifiers have two channels that can be selected either by a switch on the amp or a footswitch. One channel is usually 'clean' while the other can be driven harder to create a distorted (or 'dirty') tone. If your amp doesn't have two channels, look at the 'variation of basic controls' below to see how to get clean and dirty tones from a one channel amp.

- **Gain**
  In simple terms, the gain determines how hard you drive the amp. This governs how distorted the dirty (also called 'drive', 'overdrive', or 'distortion') channel is and acts as a second volume control on the clean channel (though a high gain setting will distort even the clean channel).

- **Bass**
  This adjusts the lowest frequencies. Boost it to add warmth and reduce or 'cut' it if your sound is muddy or woolly.

- **Middle**
  This is the most important equalisation (often shortened to just 'EQ') control. Most of the guitar's tonal character is found in the mid-range so adjusting this control has a lot of impact upon your tone. Boosting it with a dirty sound will create a more classic rock tone while cutting it will produce a more metal one.

- **Treble**
  This adjusts the high frequencies. Boost it to add brightness and cut it if the sound is too harsh or brittle.

- **Reverb**
  Short for 'reverberation'. This artificially recreates the ambience of your guitar in a large room, usually a hall. This dial controls the balance between the 'dry' (the sound without the reverb) and 'wet' (the sound with the reverb) sounds.

Variations of basic controls

The diagram above shows the most common amp controls. There are many variations to this basic setup, which can often be confusing. The following section is a breakdown of some of the other amp controls you may encounter:

- **Presence control**
  Sometimes this dial replaces the 'middle' control and other times it appears in addition to it. It adjusts the higher mid-range frequencies (those found between the 'middle' and 'treble' dials).

- **No reverb control**
  Reverb can be a nice addition to your guitar tone but it's not essential. Don't be concerned if your amp doesn't have a reverb control.

- **Volume, gain, master setup**
  Single channel amplifiers often have an extra volume control (in addition to the master volume) located next to the gain control. For clean sounds, keep the gain set low and the volume similarly low and use the master control for overall volume. If the master control is on 10 and you require more level, turn the volume control up. However, you may find that this starts to distort as you reach the higher numbers.

  To get a distorted tone, turn the volume down low and the gain up until you get the amount of distortion you require. Regulate the overall level with master volume. If the master control is on 10 and you require more level simply turn the volume up. In this case, however, you may find you lose clarity before you reach maximum.

Pickups

Entire books have been devoted to the intricacies of pickups. However, three basic pieces of information will help you understand a lot about your guitar tone:

- **Singlecoils**
  These narrow pickups are fitted to many guitars. The Fender Stratocaster is the most famous guitar fitted with singlecoils. They produce a bright, cutting sound that can sound a little thin in some situations, especially heavier styles of rock music.

- **Humbuckers**
  This type of pickup was originally designed to remove or 'buck' the hum produced by singlecoil pickups, hence the name. They produce a warm, mellow sound compared to singlecoil pickups but have a tendency to sound a little muddy in some situations. They are usually identifiable because they are twice the width of a singlecoil pickup. The Gibson Les Paul is a well-known guitar fitted with humbucking pickups.

- **Pickup location**
  Basically, pickups located near the guitar's neck will have the warmest sound and those located near the bridge will have the brightest sound.

Different types of 'dirty' tones

There are lots of different words to describe the 'dirty' guitar sounds. In fact, all the sounds are 'distortions' of the clean tone, which can be confusing when you consider there's a 'type' of distortion called 'distortion'. Below is a simplified breakdown of the three main types of dirty sounds, plus some listening material to help you through this tonal minefield:

- **Overdrive**
  This is the 'mildest' form of distortion. It can be quite subtle and only evident when the guitar is played strongly. It can also be full-on and aggressive.
  Hear it on: Cream – 'Sunshine Of Your Love', AC/DC – 'Back In Black', Oasis – 'Cigarettes and Alcohol'.

- **Distortion**
  This is usually associated with heavier styles of music. It's dense and the most extreme of the dirty tones and is usually associated with heavy styles of music.
  Hear it on: Metallica – 'Enter Sandman', Avenged Sevenfold – 'Bat Country', Bon Jovi – 'You Give Love A Bad Name'.

- **Fuzz**
  As the name implies, fuzz is a broken, 'fuzzy' sound. It was popular in the 1960s but, while still evident in certain genres, it's less common now.
  Hear it on: Jimi Hendrix Experience – 'Purple Haze', The Kinks – 'You Really Got Me'.

Guitar Notation Explained

THE MUSICAL STAVE shows pitches and rhythms and is divided by lines into measures. Pitches are named after the first seven letters of the alphabet.

TABLATURE graphically represents the guitar fingerboard. Each horizontal line represents a string and each number represents a fret.

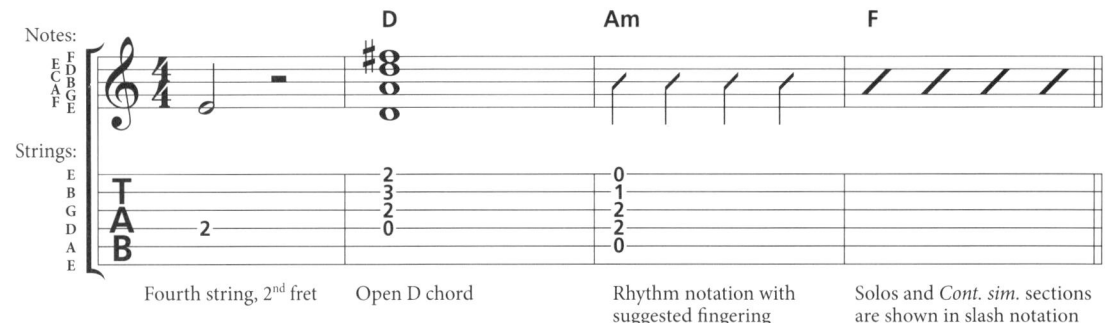

Fourth string, 2nd fret   Open D chord   Rhythm notation with suggested fingering   Solos and *Cont. sim.* sections are shown in slash notation

Definitions For Special Guitar Notation

HAMMER-ON: Pick the lower note, then sound the higher note by fretting it without picking.

PULL-OFF: Pick the higher note then sound the lower note by lifting the finger without picking.

SLIDE: Pick the first note and slide to the next. If the line connects (as below) the second note is *not* repicked.

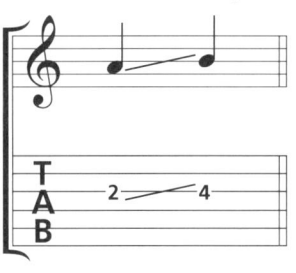

GLISSANDO: Slide off of a note at the end of its rhythmic value. The note that follows *is* repicked.

STRING BENDS: Pick the first note then bend (or release the bend) to the pitch indicated in brackets.

VIBRATO: Vibrate the note by bending and releasing the string smoothly and continuously.

TRILL: Rapidly alternate between the two bracketed notes by hammering on and pulling off.

NATURAL HARMONICS: Lightly touch the string above the indicated fret then pick to sound a harmonic.

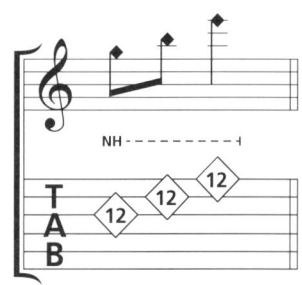

PINCHED HARMONICS: Bring the thumb of the picking hand into contact with the string immediately after the pick.

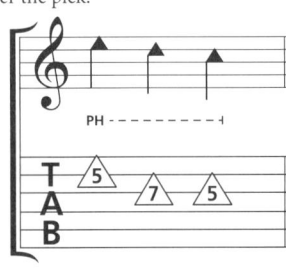

PICK-HAND TAP: Strike the indicated note with a finger from the picking hand. Usually followed by a pull-off.

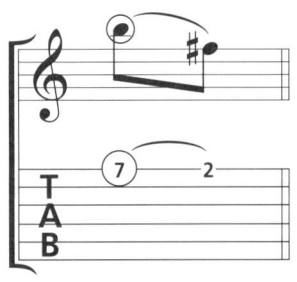

FRET-HAND TAP: As pick-hand tap, but use fretting hand. Usually followed by a pull-off or hammer-on.

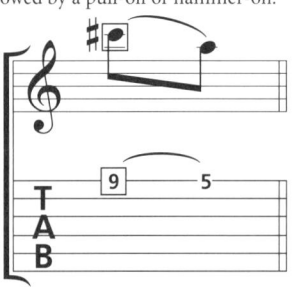

QUARTER-TONE BEND: Pick the note indicated and bend the string up by a quarter tone.

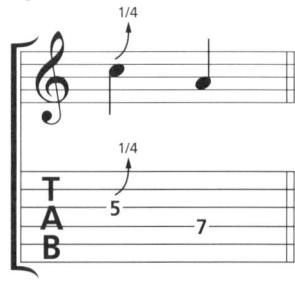

PRE-BENDS: Before picking the note, bend the string from the fret indicated between the staves, to the equivalent pitch indicated in brackets in the TAB.

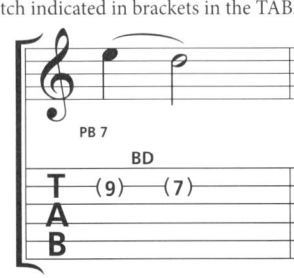

WHAMMY BAR BEND: Use the whammy bar to bend notes to the pitches indicated in brackets in the TAB.

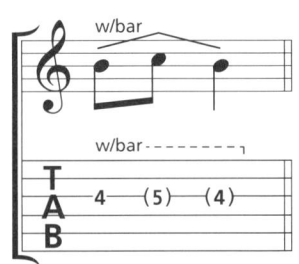

D.𝄋. al Coda

D.C. al Fine

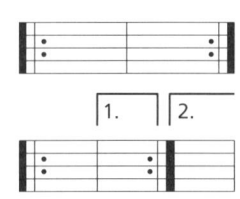

- Go back to the sign (𝄋), then play until the measure marked **To Coda** ⊕ then skip to the section marked ⊕ **Coda**.
- Go back to the beginning of the song and play until the measure marked **Fine** (end).
- Repeat the measures between the repeat signs.
- When a repeated section has different endings, play the first ending only the first time and the second ending only the second time.

Mechanical Copyright Information

Native Sons
(League)
Universal Music Publishing Limited

Die To Live
(Vai)
Carlin Music Corporation

Kid Charlemagne
(Fagen/Becker)
Universal/MCA Music Limited

Spanish Joint
(Stone/Archer/Hargrove)
Universal Music Publishing Limited/Hardgroove Publishing

Cry Me A River
(Timberlake/Storch/Mosley)
Imagem Music/Warner/Chappell North America Limited/Reservoir Media Music

Country Boy
(Lee/Colton/Smith)
Universal/Island Music Limited

mcps